SANTA FE TALES & MORE

SANTA FE TALES & MORE

HOWARD BRYAN

CLEAR LIGHT PUBLISHERS
SANTA FE, NEW MEXICO

First Edition
10 9 8 7 6 5 4 3 2 1

Library of Congress Cataloging in Publication Data

Bryan, Howard.
    Santa Fe Tales & More / by Howard Bryan --1st ed.
        p.cm.
    Includes bibliographical references and index.
    ISBN-13: 978-1-57416-095-6   ISBN-10: 1-57416-095-8

1. Santa Fe (N.M.) --History--Anecdotes.
2. Santa Fe (N.M.) --Biography--Anecdotes.
I. Title. II. Title: Santa Fe Tales and More.

F804.S257B79 2009
978.9'5604--dc22   2009010896

Book and Cover Design by Gregory Lucero
Interior Design and Typopgraphy by Gregory Lucero

Cover Photograph: Wagon trains, San Francisco Street at Plaza, Santa Fe, New Mexico, 1869 Photo by Nicholas Brown (Courtesy Museum of New Mexico Neg No. 070437)

FOREWORD

Only Howard Bryan could have written these twenty-four fun and fascinating tales of Santa Fe and New Mexico. His 40 years of in-depth research and his many interviews with pioneers who are long since gone has revealed unique items of New Mexico history. As always, he tells the stories in his own way, making them a pleasure to read while never straying from historical accuracy. He tells us what is real and what is not. Authentic history is always important to Howard and he has set straight many previously accepted "facts".

The tales lean toward the "Wild West" era most of us find so interesting. There are stories of Santa Fe's scandals, duels, robberies, and controversial citizens and visitors, from the lady gambler La Tules to Governor Lew Wallace and Billy the Kid. The reader will find many little known nuggets of Santa Fe history.

The tales go well beyond Santa Fe to include Silver City, Mesilla, and the little town of Puerto de Luna. We learn about Buffalo Bill's friend Captain Jack Crawford, "The Poet Scout", who spent many years in New Mexico. We find that the militant Apache Chief Cochise actually gave newspaper interviews back in the 1870's. There is the erroneous and amusing tale of Victorio's newspaper called The Apache Chronicle , a subscription to which cost "three scalps per noon." Scalps of soldiers, of course!

No matter how much or how little you have read about Santa Fe and New Mexico history this book will be a treat. Some tales will change what you think you know. You will find them all fascinating.

Robert G. McCubbin
President, Wild West History Association

TABLE OF CONTENTS

PART ONE

SANTA FE TALES

TABLE OF CONTENTS

PART TWO

MORE NEW MEXICO TALES

SANTA FE DAILY DEMOCRAT.

SANTA FE, N. M., FRIDAY EVENING, OCTOBER 22, 1880.

These denouements signal the utter defeat of the party in the county. That there are good men in the ranks of the republican party, no one more freely admits than we, but that they are powerless to check the persistent unmanliness of some of their less honorable followers, continued developments are fast establishing. We watch, as we wait, for the result of the political auction. The political policy shop now has a fine combination to play:

"$329"--"$200."

New Mexico.
(Special Correspondence.)

Socorro, N. M., Oct. 1—The tide of immigration is setting strongly in the direction of New Mexico. The great advantage offered by a climate that admits of outdoor work the whole year, is attracting capital and miners from the inhospitable regions of the North. Capitalists are beginning to understand that $50 ores in large deposits, that can be worked 365 days in the year, are a surer source of wealth than richer ores in narrow veins that can only be worked four out of the twelve months.

Systematic development is taking the place of superficial prospecting, with results satisfactory to the most sanguine.

The Terence Mine at Socorro,

BREAK IT!! HOW?

Vote for Miguel A. Otero and the Democratic County Ticket of Santa Fe County.

POLITICAL PECULATIONS.

Damning Facts That Defy Contradiction.

A Board of Registration for one of the Precincts Closed

Because of a too Heavy Democratic Vote Being Polled.

of the most prominent republicans on yesterday, one of their number was delegated to wait upon another republican of prominence, and influence, and he was entrusted with the following commission:—After announcing to Rep. No. 1, Rep. No. 1 proceeded to inform him of the WITHDRAWAL OF TWO NOMINEES in the persons of Mr. Irvin, candidate for School Commissioner, and Mr. Griffin candidate for County Commissioner, he proceeded to

Portion of Santa Fe Daily Democrat, Friday October 21, 1880
(Courtesy of author's collection))

INTRODUCTION

The selections in this book are based to a large extent on New Mexico history columns I wrote for the Albuquerque Tribune during the forty-two years (1948-1990) I was employed by that newspaper. Those columns, in turn, were based largely on my research through 19th century New Mexico newspapers and my interviews with New Mexico pioneers.

Early newspapers consulted included those in Santa Fe, Albuquerque, Las Vegas, Silver City, Las Cruces and Mesilla. Most can be viewed on microfilm at various locations, including the Albuquerque Publishing Company, the New Mexico Historical Society and the University of New Mexico.

Individuals who were helpful in past years include Gilberto Espinosa, Albuquerque attorney, who in 1968 furnished me with a Xerox copy of the last will and testament of Maria Gertrudis Barcelo, the lady gambler known as La Tules. Espinosa and Fray Angelico Chaves furnished information on Santa Fe's Tertio-Millenial celebration.

Carlos C. Clancey furnished information on his father, John G. Clancey, retired sea captain turned sheep rancher, and Charles Nattress furnished information on his uncle, John "Captain Jack" Crawford, the poet scout. Some examples of Native American humor were furnished by Wendell Chino, president of the Mescalero Tribe, and Kay Arviso, Navajo educator.

Books that have been helpful include: *Dona Tules, Santa Fe's Courtesan and Gambler*, by Mary J. Straw Cook, University of New Mexico Press, 2007. *Francois X. Aubry. Trailmaker and Voyageur in the Southwest*, by Donald Chaput, The Arthur H. Clark Company, 1975. *The Leading Facts of New Mexico History*, Volume II, by Ralph E. Twitchell, Horn and Wallace (reprint), 1963.

Howard Bryan

Exposition Hall at Tertio-Millennial Exposition 1883 Photo By Ben Wittick
(Courtesy of Museum of New Mexico Neg. No. 011005)

BOGUS BIRTHDAY BASH:
How Old is Santa Fe?

S anta Fe has been known as "The City Different" for many reasons; even its founding date is unclear. But that did not stop the citizens of Santa Fe from staging a major celebration in observance of what they believed to be the 333rd anniversary of their city's founding during the summer of 1883. Called the "Tertio-Millennial," meaning one-third of a thousand years, this celebration lasted 33 days and drew thousands of visitors from all parts of the nation, some arriving in chartered Pullman cars.

The celebration, which began on July 2, featured a series of colorful street parades and historical pageants depicting various phases of New Mexico's history. These pageants were staged on exposition grounds adjacent to an unfinished, stone-faced building located two blocks north of the Santa Fe plaza. Originally intended to be the territorial capital, this building instead eventually became the U.S. Courthouse Building.

More than one thousand New Mexico Indians also took part in the celebration, including Mescalero Apaches, Navajos, Utes and Pueblos. All wore their native attire, including the buckskin-clad Apaches wearing colorful war bonnets and carrying lances. Santa Fe residents took part in the pageants dressed as Spanish conquistadors, Franciscan friars and other historical figures.

In the center of town, two U.S. Infantry bands from Fort Marcy furnished martial music for the parades. A wooden exhibit hall, erected on the exposition grounds, presented displays of New Mexico's Indian crafts, historical objects, minerals and agricultural products.

Of course, the event produced many souvenirs, including commemorative coins, each bearing on one side a portrait of J.B. Lamy (erroneously identifying him as the Archbishop of New Mexico rather than the Archbishop of Santa Fe). The other side featured a picture of Santa Fe's San Miguel Chapel, with the legend, "Tertio-Millenial Anniversary Santa Fe New Mexico 1550-1883."

What Santa Fe residents did not know at the time, however, was that their Tertio-Millenial celebration was about six decades premature, for it would not be until the early 1940s that Santa Fe could count 333 years. Little was known about the history of New Mexico and Santa Fe then, and many of Santa Fe's earliest records had been destroyed during the Pueblo Revolt of 1680.

So where did they come up with the year 1550? For obscure reasons, there was a belief that Santa Fe had been founded in 1550 by deserters from the Coronado Expedition, which during the period 1540-1542 had headquartered on the Rio Grande at least sixty miles to the south. This also led to a belief that Francisco Vasquez de Coronado, commander of the expedition, had established his headquarters in an Indian pueblo on the site of Santa Fe, and that the adobe building known as "the oldest house in Santa Fe" was a part of that pueblo.

These misconceptions were corrected by noted historian Hubert Howe Bancroft in his 1889 book, *History of Arizona and New Mexico*. Bancroft was the first historian to consult the early Spanish language book, *Historia de La Nueva Mexico*, by Gaspar de Villagra, published in Spain in 1610. Villagra was among the first Spanish colonists in New Mexico.

Bancroft gave the date of Santa Fe's founding as between 1605 and 1616, although research since then places the date at about 1609, give or take a year. Documentary evidence is lacking as to the exact date of the city's founding.

Juan de Oñate, who led the first Spanish settlers into New Mexico in 1598, had established New Mexico's first capital at San Juan Pueblo (now Ohkay Owingeh) on the east bank of the Rio Grande, near present-day Española. He later moved it across the river to an abandoned pueblo the Spaniards called San Gabriel. Although Oñate

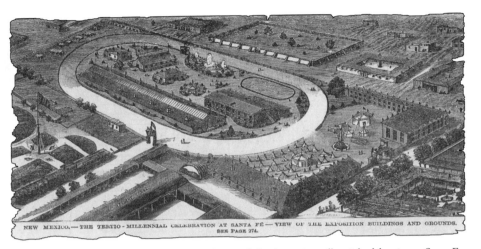

NEW MEXICO.— THE TERTIO-MILLENNIAL CELEBRATION AT SANTA FÉ — VIEW OF THE EXPOSITION BUILDINGS AND GROUNDS. SEE PAGE 274.

Birds-eye view of the exposition buildings and grounds for the tertio-millennial celebration at Santa Fe, 1875 Published by Frank Lesile's Newspaper (Courtesy Fray Angelico Chavez History Library 3-10t)

may have inaugurated plans to move the capital to a new location about thirty miles to the south, it was Pedro de Peralta, who succeeded Oñate as governor in 1609, who is credited with the founding of Santa Fe and moving the San Gabriel settlers to the new location.

In 1610, the new capital was rapidly taking shape in an uninhabited area on the banks of a small stream at the western foot of the Sangre de Cristo Mountains about twenty miles east of the Rio Grande, then known as El Rio del Norte. Over a century later, in 1779, New Mexico governor Juan Bautista de Anza decided the city should move to a new location. He chose the east bank of the Rio Grande, between Santo Domingo and Cochiti pueblos, about twenty-five miles southwest of Santa Fe. At the time this was the ranch of Nuestra Señora de Guadalupe de la Peña Blanca, occupied by the family of Jose Miguel de la Peña, the present-day village of Peña Blanca.

According to an early document, Anza believed it would be profitable to move Santa Fe to the new location "because it is a clear and spacious locality, not too cold in temperature, and much more pleasant than that of Santa Fe." The proposed site had farmlands sufficient for raising plentiful harvests of wheat and other grains, he added. Wood and lumber were plentiful in the nearby mountains, and the river would provide the necessary water for irrigation "with no expense whatsoever and very little work." This was in contrast to the Santa Fe site, which lacked sufficient irrigation water and suffered a shorter growing season.

In order to not abandon the settlement entirely, Anza recommended that at least one hundred of the approximately 1900 citizens stay at the present site; that these citizens be resettled south of the small Santa Fe River; and that all buildings north of the river be demolished. However (not surprisingly), most citizens of Santa Fe opposed the plan, and twenty-four of them fled south to complain to higher Spanish authorities, who vetoed the plan.

Although Juan Bautista de Anza was credited with founding San Francisco, California, in 1775, he was unsuccessful in his plan to found a new Santa Fe on the Rio Grande.

Spanish Captain, Juan Bautista de Anza 1774 (Courtesy of Public Domain)

Mescalero Apaches at Tertio Millenial Exposition, Santa Fe, New Mexico 1883 (Courtesy Museum of New Mexico No. 056138)

"Apache Headquarters" at Tertio Millenial Exposition, Santa Fe, New Mexico 1883 Photo by Ben Wittick (Courtesy Museum of New Mexico No. 015922)

La Dona Tules. "Gertrudis Barcelo painting of La Dona Tules at gambling table taken from New Mexico Magazine 1971 (Courtesy of author's collection)

THEY CALLED HER LA TULES
Maria Gertrudis Barcelo, Lady Gambler

If there was one thing about Maria Gertrudis Barcelo that everybody agreed upon it was the fact that "La Tules," as she was generally known, was the most expert monte dealer in Santa Fe. Maria Gertrudis Barcelo, variously known as La Tules, Dona Tules, Señora Toulous, Dona Tula and Tules (the Spanish diminutive of Gertrudis) was a controversial figure described by some as a respectable and devoutly religious woman and by others as "a female of very loose habits." Her personal life and background may have been the subject of some debate, but nobody doubted her skill with the Mexican playing cards, least of all those American traders and trappers who sometimes lost the profits of an entire season in an hour's play.

At the time of the American occupation of New Mexico in 1846, La Tules was the operator of a plush gambling salon (known as a monte bank), two blocks west of the Santa Fe plaza. The salon occupied one of four adobe buildings she owned at the present-day convergence of Palace Avenue, Burro Alley and Grant Avenue. One of them, facing east on Grant Avenue, served as her private residence.

The interior of the salon was very elegant for its time and frontier location. Machine-made Brussels carpets, hauled by wagon train down the Santa Fe Trail, covered the hard mud floors. Elaborate mirrors, also imported by wagon train, adorned the walls. Large chandeliers, each loaded with burning candles, provided the illumination.

Salon patrons included the socially elite of Santa Fe, high-ranking government officials, clergymen and military officers. Frequent dances were held in one of the richly furnished rooms for those fortunate enough to receive invitations.

While La Tules' gambling exploits are well-known, the details of her personal life are more obscure. Recent research has shown that Gertrudis Barcelo was born in about 1800 in the Mexican state of Sonora, the second of three children of Jose Ignacio Barcelo and his wife, Dolores Herrero. Gertrudis had an older brother, Jose Trinidad Barcelo, and a younger sister, Maria de la Luz Barcelo.

The Barcelo family moved north to New Mexico in about 1815, settling in the village of Valencia, on the east bank of the Rio Grande about twenty miles south of Albuquerque. Records of the Catholic Church at Tome, a neighboring settlement, show that Gertrudis Barcelo was married to Manuel Antonio Sisneros on June 23, 1823. They soon became the parents of two successive sons, both of whom died in infancy, and Gertrudis began adopting and raising several young females of uncertain parentage.

Juan Ignacio, father of Gertrudis, died shortly after the family arrived in New Mexico, and her widowed mother married Don Pedro Pino of Valencia. Her brother, Trinidad, married Dolores Griego of Corrales, just north of Albuquerque, and her sister, Maria de la Luz, married Juan Rafael Sanches, member of a prominent Tajique land grant family, and lived for years in the villages of Tajique and Manzano.

It is uncertain how Gertrudis Barcelo developed her gambling skills, but in the late 1820s she was a successful gambler at Dolores, or Old Placers, a flourishing new gold mining camp in the Ortiz Mountains south of Santa Fe. She and her husband were living in Santa Fe by 1833, where she continued her gambling career at various locations in the city. A shrewd businesswoman, she soon became one of the wealthiest citizens of Santa Fe and was running her own successful salon. Since there was no local bank, she shipped large sums of money to banks in St. Louis and elsewhere. Prominent Santa Fe citizens borrowed money from her, and she often filed suits to recover unpaid loans.

Her husband, Manuel Antonio Sisneros, disappeared from the records after 1841, and his fate remains unknown. Historian Ralph E.

Twitchell wrote that Sisneros was excommunicated by Bishop J.B. Lamy, after which he was no longer recognized by his relatives, but no verification of this claim had been found in church records. During the remainder of her career, she was said to have had a number of prominent lovers and partners, including Manuel Armijo, governor of New Mexico, and August de Marle, a Prussian-born lieutenant with the U.S. Army.

Most of what is known about La Tules and her Santa Fe gambling establishment was left to posterity by early New Mexico visitors who mentioned her in their writings. Josiah Gregg, early chronicler of the Santa Fe Trail, wrote in his book *Commerce of the Prairies* that La Tules arrived in Santa Fe in the early 1830s in search of fame and fortune and spent much of her time patronizing monte games in the gambling halls. Fortune did not smile upon her efforts at first, he wrote, and for some years she spent her days in lowliness and misery:

> *At last her luck turned, and on one occasion she left the bank with a spoil of several hundred dollars. This enabled her to open a bank of her own, and being favored with a continuous run of good fortune, she gradually rose higher and higher in the scale of affluence until she found herself in possession of a very handsome fortune.*
>
> *She is openly received in the first circles of society. I doubt, in truth, whether there is to be found in the city a lady of more fashionable reputation than this same Tules, now known as Senora Dona Gertrudis Barcelo.*

Matthew C. Field, correspondent for the New Orleans *Picayune*, wrote that he stood spellbound in 1839 as he watched La Tules in action in her monte bank. At the time, she was relieving a Kentuckian of his earnings:

"Had you looked in her countenance for any symptom by which to discover how the game stood, you would have turned away unsatisfied," he wrote, "for calm seriousness was alone discernible, and the cards fell from her fingers as steadily as though she were handling only a knitting needle."

Field, who referred to the lady gambler as "Senora Toulous," echoed the opinion of other writers that she was not a particularly attractive woman, adding that her only pleasant feature was "an eye of shrewd intelligence." But he also noted that she had a neat figure, was a graceful dancer and had a keen sense of humor.

While visiting her private home in Santa Fe, Field noticed that her wall clock, an expensive one of American manufacture, had stopped running, and commented on the fact to La Tules. He wrote that, "The señora told us facetiously that she was economical with her clock, it being too handsome to work, and not wishing it to grow old too fast, she only let it go on holidays."

John S. Forsythe, another correspondent for the New Orleans *Picayune*, claimed that La Tules lost $150,000 in gold coins that were being shipped on mules to Missouri in 1839 for deposit in eastern banks. According to this questionable story, which has some variations, La Tules hired two Santa Fe freighters, Raul Cortez and Manuel Di Grazi, to transport the money east. They reportedly packed the coins in twenty-five buckskin pouches, loaded them on the backs of ten mules, and headed northeast by way of Taos with three other packers.

Months later, Cortez struggled into Santa Fe from the south, claiming that bandits had attacked the mule train about forty miles east of Taos, and that during the battle he had buried the coins, along with two of his companions, near three large rocks, one of them half the size of a house. He said the bandits killed all his companions and took him captive after searching unsuccessfully for the money he had buried, eventually releasing him far to the south of Santa Fe. He reportedly died in Santa Fe after drawing a crude map of where the money was concealed, but, not surprisingly, all efforts to find the buried treasure were in vain.

La Tules looking over her playing cards while to gentlemen look on. (Courtesy of author's collection)

Susan Shelby Magoffin, 18-year-old bride of Santa Fe trader Samuel Magoffin, saw La Tules in Santa Fe in 1846 and described her as "the old woman with false hair and teeth" in her diary, which was published later as *Down the Santa Fe Trail and into Mexico*. The teenager wrote after seeing La Tules at a social funcion, "There was Dona Tula, the principal monte bank dealer in Santa Fe, a stately dame of certain age, the possessor of a portion of that shrewd sense and fascinating manner necessary to allure the wayward, inexperienced youth into the hall of final ruin." She also noted that the woman gambler, as well as many other Santa Fe women, smoked small cigars, called cigarrittos, consisting of a small amount of tobacco wrapped in a corn shuck, or a bit of paper.

George Douglas Brewerton, a 21-year-old U.S. Army lieutenant from New York, described La Tules as he saw her in 1848 in his book *Overland With Kit Carson*, published posthumously in 1930:

> She was richly but tastelessly dressed, her fingers being literally covered with rings, while her neck was adorned with three heavy chains of gold, to the longest of which was attached a massive crucifix of the same precious material.

He added that although she was not advanced in life, her face "was scarred and seamed and rendered unwomanly by those painful lines which unbridled passions and midnight watching never failed to stamp upon the countenance of their votary."

Historian Ralph E. Twitchell, whose knowledge of La Tules was gained through research and interviews, claimed that she was the mistress of Manuel Armijo, the last New Mexico governor under Mexican rule, and that she was "the power behind the throne." Later, he added, she became a great favorite with U.S. Army officers in Santa Fe, and was credited with coming to their rescue on several occasions.

One example of this happened in December of 1846. Learning of a conspiracy among some prominent Santa Fe residents for a Christmas Eve revolt against American rule, she informed U.S. military officials of the plot so that they could nip it in the bud. On another occasion, when U.S. troops in Santa Fe ran out of money, she agreed to a $1,000 loan to pay the troops after the commanding officer, Colonel David D. Mitchell, agreed to escort her to a fancy dress ball.

Much of what is known today about the family life and personal property of La Tules is contained in her 1850 last will and testament, which came to light in Santa Fe more than a century later. The will, written in the English language, was dated October 30, 1850, a little more than a year before her death.

Principal beneficiaries of the will were her widowed sister, Maria de la Luz Barcelo; her brother, Trinidad Barcelo; an adopted daughter, Maria del Refugio, wife of Santiago Flores, and their daughter, Delfinia; and 12-year-old Consuela de los Rayos Gutierres, known as Rallitos, born out of wedlock to Petra Gutierres prior to her 1842 marriage to James L. Giddings. Petra was another of Barcelo's adopted daughters.

The will was witnessed by some of Santa Fe's most prominent citizens, including Donaciano Vigil, former New Mexico governor; Francisco Ortiz y Delgado, mayor of Santa Fe; Manuel Alvarez, former U.S. consul, and Samuel Ellison, court clerk and territorial librarian.

This is the text of the will:

In the name of God, amen, I, Maria Gertrudis Barcelo, resident of Santa Fe in the Territory of New Mexico, being of sound mind and judgment and of the Roman Catholic faith, do hereby publish, pronounce and declare the following to be my last will and testament.

First, I declare and state that I am entirely free from debt and that the property of every kind that I am about to dispose of had been accumulated by my own labor and exertions. That this my last will and testament is irrevocable and I wish the substance and clear interpretation intent and meanings thereof to be carried out reference to any formalities or technicalities of the law. The disposition which I wish to be made of my property personal and real after my death is as follows (to wit):

First, I give and bequeath and devise unto my beloved sister, Maria de la Luz Barcelo, the house in said town of Santa Fe in which I now reside, together with all the property therein contained belonging to me, including my plate jewelry, wearing apparel and household furniture of every kind, also my carriage and the land upon which said house is situated with all the rights, privileges and appurtenances thereto belonging.

Secondly, I give devise and bequeath to Rallitos Gutierres alias Sisnero (a young girl whom I have brought up from infancy and who now resides with me) the house now occupied by Doloris Barcelo in said town of Santa Fe together with the land on which it stands and all the rights, privileges and appurtenances thereto belonging to her the said Rallitos her heirs and assigns forever in fee simple.

Third, I give, bequeath and devise unto Delfinia Flores (daughter of Santiago Flores of said town of Santa Fe) a certain other house which I own and possess in said town (at present unoccupied and west of the land last bequeathed to said Rallitos Gutierres) together with the land on which it stands and the rights, privileges and appurtenances thereto belonging to her the said Delfinia her heirs and assigns forever in fee simple.

Fourth, I give and bequeath unto my said sister Maria de la Luz Barcelo and my brother, Trinidad Barcelo, who are my heirs at law, my stock of mules to be equally divided between them, one half to each.

Fifth, I give bequeath and devise unto my said brother Trinidad and my sister Maria de la Luz and Refugio (the wife of said Santiago Flores) all the money I may possess and what may be recovered from those who owe me at the time of my death, to be divided in equal proportions between them, to each one third part of the same after paying my funeral expenses.

Provided that the above devises made hereby to said Refugio and, Delfinia Flores are made and given on the express condition that said Santiago Flores shall maintain, educate, clothe and support the said Rallitos Gutierres and another girl who resides with me called Carmel Sisnero from the time of my death until they arrive at the age of twenty five years (if not previously married) otherwise to the time of their marriage and no longer.

The above devises are hereby made to the above named parties absolutely and without restriction except as above provided, the land and real property in fee simple and the personal property absolutely, reserving to the church and government their rights, if any they have under the existing laws, to the church thirty dollars for each demand should the existing laws require.

Top painting: Depicts men in suits and hats seated at a gaming table with La Tules center of the action. by B. Houghes (Courtesy of author's collection)

And finally, I hereby nominate constitute and appoint Augustus De Marle, Gaspar Ortis and the reverend Juan Felipe Ortis my executors and charge them to faithfully carry out and perform the foregoing provisions, and to conclude do now declare, publish and pronounce the same to be my last will and testament, as witness my hand and seal this thirtieth day of October in the year of Our Lord one thousand eight hundred and fifty.

(Signed) Maria Gertrudis Barcelo.

The lady gambler known as La Tules died in Santa Fe on January 17, 1852. She was buried with the highest honors of her church in the south chapel of the parish church, site of the present St. Francis Cathedral.

Shortly after Barcelo's death, Rallitos, the young girl who inherited her residence, was married at age fourteen to Lorenzo Labadie, pioneer New Mexico Indian agent, and the residence was soon occupied by the Santa Fe *Weekly Gazette.*

Francis X. Aubry (Courtesy of Public Domain)

FASTER THAN THE TELEGRAPH
Francis X. Aubry

Handsome, a boon companion and a dashing cavalier, popular among men and more popular among women, equally at home on a dance floor or in a boxing ring, and a dead shot with a pistol or rifle.

That's how a Santa Fe pioneer described Francis X. Aubry, an energetic and adventurous young French-Canadian who considered Santa Fe his home base during the last years of his short and remarkable life as a trader, trail blazer, journalist and record-setting horseback rider on the Santa Fe Trail. Physically he was described as a slender young man of medium build with dark hair and eyes and a well-trimmed mustache and beard.

Although Aubry never established a permanent residence in Santa Fe (except perhaps for a prairie schooner), he was in and out of the city at frequent intervals during the period from 1846 to 1854 during his extensive journeys throughout the American Southwest and beyond.

Born Francois Xavier Aubry in 1824 on a farm in the province of Quebec, Canada, he was the eldest of nine children of Joseph and Magdeleine Lupien Aubry. He was baptized at the nearby village of Maskinonge, and attended local schools.

In 1843, at the age of nineteen, he left home for the United States and employment at a dry goods store in St. Louis, Missouri, operated by: the French-Canadians Moise Lamoureux and Elzear Blanchard. Here he learned to speak English, and his given name was anglicized to Francis, occasionally Frank. His father died while he was working in St. Louis, and he sent part of his wages home to his mother. He would continue to provide financial aid to her and his brothers during the remainder of his life.

Aubry's enthusiasm and inventiveness made him an immediate success in his new homeland. He became involved in the bustling Santa Fe trade at the outbreak of the Mexican War in the spring of 1846, when he obtained credit from his employers, purchased trade goods, and paid Santa Fe traders James Webb and George Doan $117 to ship the goods to Santa Fe on their wagon train. He accompanied the wagon train on the 800-mile trip down the Santa Fe Trail from Independence, Missouri, to Santa Fe, arriving on June 23, 1846, when he sold his goods at a profit estimated at several thousand dollars.

Aubry remained in Santa Fe until July 16 when he returned to Missouri with a group of traders, arriving in St. Louis on August 22. It was during this trip that he began keeping detailed journals of his observations that were published in various newspapers.

In the spring of 1847 he raised $6,000, with which he purchased his own wagons, mules and supplies for the Santa Fe trade. Arriving in Santa Fe in July, he not only sold his merchandise at a profit, but also sold his wagons and mules for a reported $6,000. He left Santa Fe on July 28 with a wagon train that was headed east, but left the train in Kansas to race ahead on horseback, reaching Independence on August 31, covering the last 300 miles in four days.

Aubry had become tired of the slow pace of this travel. At a time when wagon trains were making one trip to Santa Fe each summer season, he realized that he could double or triple his profits by taking two or three caravans to Santa Fe each year. He accomplished this by quickly selling his merchandise in Santa Fe, sometimes including the wagons and draft animals, then racing back to Independence on relays of horses and mules that he stationed at intervals along the trail or bought from passing caravans.

Land speed records for this distance began to fall, in spite of obstacles and bad luck that would have derailed a lesser adventurer. Aubry arrived back in Santa Fe with his second caravan on October 29, 1847, sold his merchandise, then raced back to Independence in fourteen days, setting a new speed record for the distance even though he was stopped and robbed by bandits along the way and killed three mules by hard riding. Early in 1848 he broke his own speed record by racing from Santa Fe to Independence in eight days and ten hours, despite the fact that he was captured briefly by Comanches and robbed of his animals, and walked forty miles to Fort Mann, in western Kansas, where he bought a fresh mount.

During his frequent visits to Santa Fe, Aubry became acquainted with the brothers Henri and Joseph Mercure, fellow French-Canadians from Quebec, who operated a combination mercantile store and saloon in the middle of the block on the south side of the plaza. The brothers became Aubry's closest friends, and their establishment became like a second home to the young adventurer.

While visiting with friends in the Mercure saloon in September, 1848, Aubry said he was willing to bet a large sum of money, said to have ranged from $1,000 to $5,000, that he could ride his relay of horses to Independence in six days. His boast was greeted with laughter. All clamored for "easy money," and Aubry covered all bets.

At dawn on September 12, 1848, Aubry left Santa Fe astride his favorite horse, a yellow mare named Dolly, and leading several other lightly saddled horses. During his 780-mile race up the Santa Fe Trail he encountered 24 hours of steady rain, swollen rivers and miles of mud. He walked twenty miles, ate six meals, and slept two and one-half hours while strapped to his saddle.

Completely exhausted, and having to be lifted from his saddle, Aubry arrived in Independence on the evening of September 17, having completed the difficult journey in five days and sixteen hours, a trail record never to be matched or exceeded. According to some reports, he pocketed an estimated $20,000 in bets.

Having set what he knew was an unbeatable record, Aubry was ready to move on to another adventure. He continued on to St. Louis by river steamer and coach, arriving in St. Louis just ten days after leaving Santa Fe. Upon his arrival, he handed a letter of introduction to the editor of a St. Louis newspaper, from the editor of the Santa Fe *Republican*, which began, "Allow me to introduce you to the man to whom the telegraph is a fool." Due to his incredible speed and endurance, Aubry was often referred to as "Telegraph Aubry" and "skimmer of the plains."

Among those witnessing a brief portion of Aubry's record-breaking horseback ride was Alexander Majors, a Santa Fe trader who a dozen years later was one of the founders of the Pony Express mail delivery service between St. Joseph, Missouri, and Sacramento, California. Aubry's relay rides are believed to have been the inspiration for the Pony Express relay system for horseback riders carrying the mail quickly across long distances.

Although he never embarked on such record-breaking rides again, Aubry continued to operate wagon trains on the Santa Fe Trail, accompanied by his personal servant, a free black man named Pompey, and his prize yellow mare, Dolly. He soon became fluent in Spanish, as well as the English and French languages.

Aubry's wagon trains did not operate without tragedy. Joining an Aubry caravan to Santa Fe in the fall of 1849 was James M. White, a prominent Santa Fe merchant, together with his wife, Mrs. Ann Dunn White; their eight-year-old daughter, Virginia; a black female servant, and thirteen wagonloads of merchandise. When they were about a week out of Santa Fe, White decided to leave the caravan and rush on ahead to Santa Fe with his wife, daughter and servant girl. They were joined by six men from the caravan, and all left in two carriages.

Leaving the relative safety of the wagon train turned out to be a fatal mistake. On the morning of October 25, 1849, while camped at a spring near an outcrop known as Point of Rocks in northeast New Mexico, the White party was attacked by about one hundred Jicarilla Apaches, who killed all the men in the group. Taken captive were

Mrs. White, her young daughter, and the servant girl. Aubry offered a $1,000 reward for their rescue.

A military force, guided by Christopher "Kit" Carson, located and attacked the Apache camp on November 17, at which time Mrs. White was killed by the Apaches. No trace of her daughter and the female servant was ever found, although some believe that Virginia White lived for many years among the Jicarilla Apaches and died as an elderly woman under the name Mrs. Marguerita Inez at Dulce, New Mexico.

Aubry was constantly trying new routes in an effort to save time. Testing a new trade route in 1849 and 1850, Aubry took his wagons south to Chihuahua, Mexico, and east across Texas from El Paso to San Antonio and beyond to Victoria, near the Texas gulf coast. Returning to the familiar Santa Fe Trail, he made three trips from Missouri to Santa Fe in 1852, making use of the Aubry Cut-off, a shortcut he had blazed the year before in southwest Kansas that shortened the trail by about fifty miles.

Looking for a new source of adventure and profit, Aubry next turned his attention to California, which was experiencing a population explosion as a result of the 1849 gold rush. The mining camp boom brought a demand for meat and wool, among other products, and New Mexico's Hispanic ranchers and nomadic Navajos grazed thousands of sheep that could be sold at huge profits on the West Coast.

Aubry bought 5,000 head of sheep from the Navajos and assembled a caravan that included ten wagons, two hundred horses and mules, and a crew of about sixty men. The caravan left Santa Fe on November 16, 1852, driving the sheep down the Rio Grande Valley before veering southwest to Tucson and continuing west through southern Arizona to California.

The sheep caravan reached Los Angeles in mid-March, 1853, shortly after Aubry had sold 1,000 head of old and lame sheep and some of his mules to some settlers near San Bernardino for $13,000. Heading north from Los Angeles, the caravan reached San Francisco late in April, where Aubry quickly sold the remaining 4,000 sheep for $10 a head and then sold his wagons and draft animals as well, realizing a profit of $70,000.

Not content with this, Aubry turned his attention in yet another direction. He decided to return to Santa Fe across uncharted regions of northern Arizona (part of New Mexico at the time) to determine if the route were suitable for a proposed transcontinental railroad. For this wagonless trek across little known country, he assembled a party of eighteen men and thirty pack mules and horses.

Most of the men in this party had accompanied Aubry to California on the southern route. They included William Baskerville and Dick Williams, Aubry's foremen and wagonmasters; Pompey, his personal servant; Pinckney R. Tully, a Santa Fe lawyer; Francisco Guzman, also of Santa Fe; Abner E. Adair, an Aubry friend from Missouri, and a man identified only as Mr. Hendrey.

Leaving San Francisco on June 20, 1853, the party headed south to Tejon Pass, north of Los Angeles, then headed east across California to the Colorado River, which they crossed in late July. Continuing east in what proved to be a near disastrous trek across northern Arizona, the group reached Albuquerque on September 10 and arrived in Santa Fe four days later, having covered nearly 1100 miles in eighty-seven days.

The Santa Fe *Gazette*, edited by James L. Collins, published a lengthy article on September 17 telling of Aubry's arrival in the city and detailing his adventurous trip. The article began: "We take great pleasure in being able to announce to our readers the arrival of our enterprising fellow citizen, F.X. Aubry, after an arduous and perilous trip from California by a new and hitherto untraveled route." The article went on to give Aubry's account of the journey that nearly cost the eighteen men their lives.

Aubry told the newspaper that it took five days to raft their baggage and swim their horses and mules across the Colorado River, and that members of the party discovered gold nuggets on the east bank of the river. As they continued east from the river they were harassed for several days by Indians who shot arrows at them, slightly wounding Aubry and a number of animals, including Aubry's mare, Dolly.

The article referred to these Indians as *Garroteros*, a Spanish word meaning those who beat with clubs, as the weapons they used consisted of clubs and bows and arrows. The Garreteros may have been the Mojaves, a warlike tribe of the Yuman Indian family that inhabited the Colorado River Basin.

On the morning of August 14, the Aubry party paused for breakfast atop a small hill near a Garrotero village and were soon joined by about fifty friendly-seeming men, women and children from the village. As Aubry and his men were preparing to leave, however, the Indians suddenly attacked them with clubs and rocks, the women wielding clubs ranging from 18 to 24 inches long that had been concealed in the deerskin clothing of the children.

About two hundred more Garroteros then appeared and joined the action, fighting with bows and arrows as well as clubs. Aubry and his men managed to fight them off with their Colt revolvers, killing an estimated twenty-five of them and wounding others. Nearly all of Aubry's men suffered wounds, twelve of them wounded severely, and Aubry said he himself was wounded in six places. All managed to survive, however. Aubry added that Francisco Guzman and Mr. Hendrey "greatly distinguished themselves" in the battle.

This was not the end of their troubles, however. The wounded men and animals continued to struggle east across northern Arizona and soon ran out of food and water. In order to survive, they found it necessary to kill their animals for food.

"Among the animals thus eaten was Mr. Aubry's fine mare, Dolly, for which he had been offered $800 in California," the newspaper said. "She had carried him some thousands of miles and through many scenes of danger, and then rendered the last service by giving her own life to sustain that of her master."

Aubry said that on August 27, they met some Tonto Apaches, who furnished them with some meat. He added that these Indians carried in pouches small lumps of gold that they used for bullets, having no other use for them. He and his men obtained from $1,000 to $2,000 worth of gold from them in exchange for trifling articles of old clothing.

The group finally reached Zuni Pueblo on September 6, where they were well received and furnished with provisions. They reached Albuquerque on September 10, and arrived in Santa Fe four days later.

In addition to Aubry's account of his trip from California, the Santa Fe *Gazette* also published this article on September 17:

> *A day or two since we received a package from our friend, F.X. Aubry, who has lately returned from California. The package was handsomely put up to our address, and marked "a present." Of course we expected to find something that would excite the curiosity and admiration of our friends, as we knew Mr. Aubry generally acquitted himself in a becoming manner in matters of this kind.*
>
> *We carefully unfolded the package, when our curiosity was startled at the sight of, not a live Garrotero Indian, but the scalp of one folded up in its long, flowing locks of hair. We quietly replaced the envelope, remarking to ourself that the chap who had worn that "waked up the wrong passenger" when he startled*

Flock of sheep New Mexico 1925 (Courtesy of Museum of New Mexico Neg. No. 134593)

Aubry. We have since learned that our present was taken from an Indian that was killed in the battle of the 14th of August, mentioned in another column.

During his pause in Albuquerque on September 10, Aubry had visited with Richard H. Weightman, a lawyer and former New Mexico delegate to Congress, who had recently moved there from Santa Fe to establish what proved to be a short-lived weekly newspaper called *Amigo del Pais.* During their meeting, Aubry promoted the route he had just completed as the most suitable railroad route west to Los Angeles. Weightman, however, favored a more southern route through El Paso and Tucson.

Aubry did not linger in Santa Fe long, as on October 10, 1853, he headed back to California with a caravan of 50,000 sheep, of which he owned one-third. The remaining sheep were owned by Judge Antonio Jose Otero, J. Francisco Chaves, Jose Francisco Perea and Miguel Salazar, prominent New Mexico residents who accompanied Aubry on the long trek. The caravan, taking the southern route through Tucson and Los Angeles, reached San Francisco in February, 1854, where the sheep were sold.

While in California, Aubry learned that Weightman had published an article in his Albuquerque newspaper severely criticizing him and his claims of having found a more feasible railroad route to California than the southern route Weightman favored.

Furious, Aubry decided to test his route again, traveling light this time. He and his companions left San Francisco on July 1 and retraced Aubry's northern route from Tejon Pass to Albuquerque without encountering any major problems, They took with them just one wagon, upon which was a boat that they used to cross the Colorado River.

Aubry reached Santa Fe on horseback at about two o'clock in the afternoon on August 18, 1854. He rode at once to the Mercure brothers' store and saloon on the plaza, tied his horse outside, and walked inside where he was greeted by friends.

Seated at the southeast corner of the plaza at the time was Weightman, whose Albuquerque newspaper had folded after only a few months of publication. Seeing Aubry entering the saloon, he walked down the street, entered it, and shook hands with Aubry in a friendly manner.

Aubry, who was standing at a counter drinking a toddy, invited Weightman to join him for a drink. Weightman declined the invitation and sat down on the counter facing Aubry. Aubry asked him what had happened to his newspaper, and Wieghtman replied that it had died for a lack of subscribers.

"Any such lying paper ought to die," Aubry responded. Weightman asked him what he meant by that remark.

"Last fall you asked me for information about my trip, which I gave you, and you afterwards abused me," Aubry said. Weightman replied that it was not so, and Aubry slammed his fist down on the counter and exclaimed, "I say it is so!"

Weightman got off the counter, picked up a tumbler about one-third full of liquor and water and pitched the contents into Aubry's face. His eyes smarting from the liquid, Aubry reached for his Colt five-shooter, which he wore on his left side, and was attempting to cock it when it fired prematurely, sending a bullet into the ceiling. At the same moment, Weightman drew a Bowie knife from his belt and plunged it into Aubry's abdomen.

Aubry collapsed into the arms of a bystander, Santa Fe merchant Henry Cuniffe, gasping "Let me bleed." Hurrying to the scene was Dr. David C. DeLeon, a U.S. Army surgeon at nearby Fort Marcy, but his aid was in vain. Aubry died on the saloon floor within ten minutes of the stabbing. It was the third day of December, about four months short of what would have been his 30th birthday.

A large crowd attended Aubry's funeral the next day in Santa Fe's Parroquial Church, an adobe structure a short distance east of the plaza that later was demolished and replaced on the site by St. Francis Cathedral. The Santa Fe *Gazette* indicated that he was buried in the church, but church historians believe that it is more likely that he was buried in what was then a cemetery adjacent to the church, now an attractive park along the north side of the cathedral.

Weightman, quickly indicted on a murder charge, was a 36-year-old Maryland native who as a young man was expelled from the U.S. Military Academy at West Point for allegedly slashing another cadet with a knife. After moving to St. Louis, he came to Santa Fe during the Mexican War with the Missouri Light Artillery.

Discharged in 1849 with the rank of major, he remained in Santa Fe, where he practiced law and soon became embroiled in a bitter dispute with New Mexico Chief Justice Joab Houghton that was climaxed by what proved to be a harmless duel. Active in politics, he served as a New Mexico delegate to Congress in 1851-52.

A Santa Fe jury acquitted Weightman of the murder charge on September 21 1854, on grounds of self-defense. Reportedly grief-stricken over his killing of Aubry, and saying that he could always see the dead man's face before his eyes, Weightman left Santa Fe a week later and returned to his former St. Louis home. At the outbreak of the Civil War, he joined a Confederate force, the Missouri State Guard, rose to the rank of colonel and was killed in action while leading a Confederate charge at the Battle of Wilson's Creek on July 10, 1861.

Named co-administrators of Aubry's estate were Joseph Mercure and J. Francisco Chaves. The principal beneficiary was Aubry's widowed mother, then living at Trois-Rivieras, Quebec, whom Aubry had been supporting for years. He also was financing a college education for three of his younger brothers at St. Louis University.

Succeeding Mercure and Chaves as administrators of the estate in 1859 was Father Joseph Machebeuf, a native of France who was serving as vicar-general to Bishop J.B. Lamy of Santa Fe. There was $17,200 remaining in the estate at the time, and Machebeuf pressured Mrs. Aubry for a $10,000 loan for church building projects in Santa Fe.

The mercantile store and saloon that the Mercure brothers operated on the Santa Fe plaza fell on hard times following Aubry's death.

Many citizens avoided the establishment, due to the tragedy that had occurred there, and Texas troops that occupied Santa Fe during the Civil War reportedly appropriated supplies from the store when they retreated from the city in 1862.

Joseph Mercure suffered a mental breakdown early in 1863 and soon began suffering delusions of grandeur. On November 21, 1863, the Santa Fe *New Mexican* published this account of his growing insanity and death:

> *Last summer his mind began to give evident signs of becoming infected with insanity. He had ever been noted, in this city, for his sober, industrious and rather studious habits.*
>
> *Rather early in the summer he began to exhibit an excessive egotism, founded upon an impression that he was a man of great astronomical genius, and had invented a kind of solar compass surpassing anything before known in simplicity and accuracy. He believed the invention would yield him immense wealth.*
>
> *He then passed to the impression that he owned gold mines fabulous in value. Diamonds and all precious stones filled his possessions. Santa Fe was to shortly receive, on account of his mines, a population exceeding New York.*
>
> *His hallucinations then took another turn. He announced himself the second Saviour that had been sent to the Jews.*
>
> *His mind then turned to a political wildness. He proclaimed New Mexico a state, and federal authority ended here. Contended he was president of the Republic, and gave orders, verbally and in writing, to civil and military officers, and upon finding himself not obeyed, he declared them removed.*

San Miguel Church, Santa Fe, New Mexico, May 1887
(Courtesy Muesum of New Mexico Neg. No. 010082

Finally, it was thought best to confine him, for he became violent and dangerous from his temper. His brother then made excellent arrangements for his removal to an asylum in the states to be treated. On the road he died, and was buried upon the banks of the Arkansas River. His brother then sent for the body to be dishumed and brought here for final repulture.

The newspaper said that the remains of Joseph Mercure were buried within Santa Fe's San Miguel Church on November 14, 1863. His brother, Henri, served as an agent to Ute Indians in Rio Arriba County, north of Santa Fe, where he died in 1872, leaving a wife and six children.

Aubry's life and death were recalled by J. Francisco Chaves in an article published in the Albuquerque *Daily Citizen* on November 13, 1893. He wrote that Aubry was "as brave as a lion and a man of wonderful endurance," and that the Mercure brothers' store on the Santa Fe plaza, where Aubry met his death, "is now occupied by W.A. McKenzie as a hardware store." The Charles Ilfeld Co. also is said to have occupied the property for years.

The route Aubry pioneered and promoted from Albuquerque to Los Angeles was eventually used, with some variations, by the Santa Fe Railway, U.S. Highway 66 and Interstate 40.

San Francisco Street at Shelby Street, stagecoach coming into the Plaza, Santa Fe, New Mexico 1885 (Courtesy Museum of New Mexico Neg. No. 010672)

STAGECOACH DAYS IN SANTA FE

Recollections Of L.C. Wardwell

It was in the late summer of 1857 that 18-year-old Louis C. "Sandy" Wardwell and two male companions arrived on foot in Santa Fe after a twelve-day trek from Fort Union and began looking for work. For Wardwell, his arrival in Santa Fe was to mark the beginning of a long career as a New Mexico stagecoach driver, a career he later detailed in a series of eleven articles published in 1897 in the Albuquerque *Weekly News*.

Wardwell had left his Wisconsin home months before and had journeyed by riverboats on the Wisconsin, Mississippi and Missouri rivers to Westport, Missouri, eastern terminus of the Santa Fe Trail. There he got a job as the driver of ten yoke of Texas steers on a wagon train headed down the trail to Fort Union, New Mexico, about 100 miles northeast of Santa Fe. Upon reaching the fort, Wardwell and his two unidentified companions decided to walk on down the trail to Santa Fe with a sick and slow-moving burro they had bought.

"At the place which now is the town of Watrous, old Sam Tipton had a factory for the making of buckskin clothes and we all bought buckskin suits," Wardwell wrote. "On the way to Santa Fe it rained on us two or three times so that one day our clothes would be all stretched out, and next day in the sunshine they would draw up so that we could scarcely wear them. By the time we got to Santa Fe our buckskin clothes were nothing but strings."

Wardwell's first occupation in Santa Fe was certainly not something he had originally planned. He wrote that he and his friends rented a room in Santa Fe. Unable to find work, and considering themselves pretty fair comedians, they decided to stage a minstrel show. They began by getting hold of a man who worked for Joe Hersch's flour mill who could play two tunes on the fiddle, "Rorrah O'Moore" and "The Arkansas Traveler."

"I rattled the bones and my partner beat the tambourine," Wardwell wrote. "Another boy held an old guitar in his hand, while still another had the jawbone of a horse with all the teeth in, and he would take a stick across them and it would make a terrible rattling. Another boy played the triangle, and another acted as middleman."

The group rented space for the minstrel show in what was then the courthouse, opposite the northeast corner of the Santa Fe plaza, which Wardwell wrote was later occupied by Johnson and Koch as a dry goods store.

Operating a stagecoach route between Santa Fe and El Paso at the time were Tom Bowler and Frank Green, who also were proprietors of the Exchange (La Fonda) Hotel in Santa Fe. Wardwell, who mistakenly referred to Tom Bowler as Tom Bowles in his articles, wrote that he composed a song about the stagecoach route for the minstrel show that mentioned every station along the route.

In his 1897 articles, Wardwell recalled the first five verses of his song:

> A passenger said that he was bound,
>
> To get on the fastest coach above ground,
>
> He was recommended to Bowler and Green,
>
> As the fastest this country had ever seen.
>
> The passenger then jumped on board,
>
> And off they started down the road,
>
> And Pino's ranch -- it soon is seen,
>
> Hurrah, hurrah for Bowler and Green
>
> At Algodones they change the team,
>
> And off they start adown the stream,
>
> The horses fresh, oh how they snort,

As they glide along the Rio del Norte.
At Alameda they stop some time.
And take a drink of pure grape wine,
Then Albuquerque heaves in sight,
Before the day is changed to night."

Sung after each verse was the chorus:

"Then don't go 'way from Bowler and Green,
Then don't go 'way from Bowler and Green.
Then don't go 'way from Bowler and Green,
"They're the fastest the country has ever seen."

Wardwell wrote that the stagecoach company printed copies of his song before the show opened and distributed them to the stations along the line. The company also provided a portable stage, drawn by six mules, which carried the minstrel troupe around the streets of Santa Fe for two or three days before the show opened.

"On the opening night I sang the song," Wardwell wrote. "Frank Green and Tom Bowler were present. One would toss a $20 gold piece on the stage and then the other as the song proceeded, until at its close, I had $80 in gold at my feet." Wardwell wrote that he also received two $20 gold pieces from Bob Stapleton, operator of a stagecoach station south of Socorro, since the song mentioned his station and bill of fare.

The commander of Fort Marcy in Santa Fe marched a company of soldiers to the show each evening, to the accompaniment of fife and drum, and paid for them at the door at one dollar a head.

"In short, the show was a big success, and we made in seven nights $1800," Wardwell wrote. "Of course, we had a treasurer to take care of the money. Sunday night we were out serenading and got pretty full. When we met again, our treasurer did not answer the roll call, nor to this date have I seen him. We were flat broke and had to disband."

Following the close of the minstrel show, Wardwell held a variety of odd jobs with wagon outfits and private individuals, both in and out of Santa Fe, for several years. He also lived through some peculiar adventures.

"I went to Taos [in 1860] to work for a man named Colonel Means, who was married to a mulatto woman," Wardwell wrote. "I could not get along with her, so I went back to Santa Fe and went to work in a shoe shop cobbling shoes." Colonel Thomas Means, a government surveyor, apparently did not get along with his wife, either. Jailed on a charge of abusing and threatening to kill her, as well as a few other Taos residents, he was taken from his place of confinement by masked men on the night of January 2, 1867, and hanged in the adjoining courtroom.

Wardwell wrote that Tom Cotton, a monte dealer at Santa Fe's Exchange Hotel, was the best pistol shot he ever saw:

> He would stand out on the plaza in Santa Fe and let you throw up a silver dollar, and for every one he missed he would give you a $5 gold piece, and every one he hit was his. But I never saw anyone get a gold piece, for he hit them all.

Wardwell added that Cotton bet Ned Pointer a champagne supper that he could shoot the heel off one of the boots of a man who was walking across the plaza. He fired, and the man grabbed his heel and screamed with pain. It was then learned that the man was wearing moccasins, rather than boots, and had suffered a flesh wound. Cotton summoned a doctor, who dressed the wound, and gave the injured man a $20 gold piece.

A multiple lynching near Santa Fe (of which there appears to be no official record) was described by Wardwell in his 1897 recollections. The five victims, he wrote, were accused of the 1859 murder and robbery of Thomas Rowland, an elderly storekeeper in the Pecos River village of San Miguel, about 40 miles southeast of Santa Fe. Rowland's Mexican wife allegedly entered into a conspiracy with five local men to rob her husband.

"She let them in, and the old white-headed man made a fight, and they killed him," Wardwell wrote. "He had 27 knife wounds and eleven bullet holes in him."

Rowland was a veteran Freemason, and Wardwell joined a group of Santa Fe men who collected his remains and transported them to Santa Fe, where they were buried in the Masonic and Odd Fellows Cemetery a few blocks north of the plaza.

Later, Wardwell wrote that Rowland's wife and the murderers had a falling out over the division of the spoils, and she revealed the details of the murder and robbery. Five San Miguel men were arrested and charged with the murder, he wrote, but were cleared when taken to Santa Fe for trial. He continued:

> *Their friends mounted them over good horses and started them for home. Well, they had to ride around the plaza in Santa Fe and taunt the Gringos for a while, and then they galloped off, and like a pack of damn fools, they rode under some piñon trees about seven or eight miles from Santa Fe and got fastened some way. They must have not seen the ropes that were hanging there, and by some damn foolishness got tangled there.*

Wardwell was quiet about his part, if any, in this episode.

By 1864, Wardwell was involved with his primary occupation, driving stagecoaches. He wrote that he was driving for Cornelius B. "Con" Cosgrove between Santa Fe and Albuquerque in 1864, when he was asked in August to take a coach from Socorro to El Paso and back.

"At that time Cochise was the Apache chief, and he was making it very lively for the stage boys," he wrote. "I lost several of my boon companions by the Apaches."

The trip south to El Paso was uneventful, he wrote, but on the return trip north, upon reaching Fort Selden north of Las Cruces, word was received that the Apaches had raided the village of Paraje, about 90 miles to the north, and had run off all the stage stock. In spite of the warnings, a small train, led by the Wardwell's stagecoach, headed on north up the desert trail known as the Jornada del Muerto towards Paraje, on the east bank of the Rio Grande near Fort Craig.

Wardwell wrote that he had five passengers in his coach at the head of the procession. Riding in a four-mule ambulance immediately behind him was Epifanio Aguirre of Las Cruces, along with his wife, two children and two servants. A good saddle horse accompanied the ambulance. Bringing up the rear was an escort of eight soldiers with some wagons.

At daybreak on the third day out, the small caravan was attacked by several hundred Apaches at a trail landmark known as the Big Laguna.

Wardwell described the running battle:

> There was one Indian who had an old musket, and he would get down off his pony and shoot at the team. They knew, and so did I, that if they could stop us they had us dead to rights. But I was on my job, as the fellow says, and when the old devil would down a mule, I would jump down and cut it loose and keep going.

> This man Aguirre would take a six-shooter in each hand and his bridle reins in his teeth and make a dash on ahead and open the way for us, empty his pistols and dart back to his carriage, and his wife would hand him two more loaded. I never saw a man with more nerve in my life. He fought like a demon, and the escort fought well. The passengers were firing all the time, and the top of the coach looked like a porcupine's back, it was so full of arrows.

Well, we fought our way to within about six miles of Paraje, and then they gave it up and left us. I got into the station with three mules in the lead and none on the tongue. In those days we worked five mules, three in the lead and two at the tongue.

This was a pretty close call for all of us, and I think this Aguirre was the means of saving the whole outfit, for he kept the Apaches from closing in on us in the lead, and the soldiers kept them from the rear.

Epifanio Aguirre, of Spanish and Basque descent, was born in 1834 in Chihuahua, Mexico, where his father owned large haciendas. The family moved to Las Cruces in 1852. Epifanio and two of his brothers operated wagon trains on the Santa Fe Trail and elsewhere. He was killed in an Apache ambush near the Arizona-Sonora border in 1870.

Wardwell continued driving stagecoaches for several years. It was in the late 1860s, He wrote, that Judge John M. Shaw, a former Socorro preacher, obtained a mail contract from Barlow, Sanderson & Co., but lacked the money to buy a coach. He asked Wardwell to rig up the best way he could and take the mail route between Santa Fe and Albuquerque.

Wardwell wrote that he managed to buy twelve good horses and an ambulance at a government sale, had the ambulance remodeled, then started out to run the opposition out of business on the route. Here is how he did it, in his own words:

Stage fare from Santa Fe to Albuquerque was $15. Under the new program, I put it down to $10. The opposition replied to this by reducing it to $8, which I followed by a come-down to $5.

The opposition then reduced to $2.50, which I effectually countered by making the fare on my line free, with a good dinner thrown in at Algodones. Little John Miller kept the station at Algodones.

"Well, the opposition did not last long. Al Shelby sold out in about three months after I started, and I carried out the contract and then went to driving for Joe Bennett.

Wardwell drove coaches for Joseph F. Bennett until May 1, 1872, when he opened what he said was Santa Fe's first livery stable. A few months later, on August 8, he married the widowed daughter of Captain Clifford, a member of General Gordon Granger's staff in Santa Fe. He took his father-in-law in as a partner in the Wardwell & Clifford Livery Stables.

Wardwell sold the business to his partner in 1873 and moved to Cimarron, New Mexico, where he took charge of livestock for the Maxwell Land Grant Co., the Ute Indian Agency and a stagecoach line.

In following years, Wardwell and his wife, with a growing family, lived in various communities throughout New Mexico and Colorado. Sickness struck his family while he was working at Fort Craig, he wrote, and he buried four of his sons at San Marcial, a short distance north of the fort.

Eventually, the Wardwells moved to Albuquerque, where he worked in the 1890s as a hack driver. Wardwell and his wife had moved to Barstow, California, by 1910, the year one of their sons, Louis C. Wardwell Jr., was killed in an Albuquerque construction accident.

Wardwell's lengthy recollections in the Albuquerque *Weekly News* in 1897 were written anonymously, but his frequent references to himself as Sandy prompted some Albuquerque pioneers in the 1960s to positively identify him.

Street Scene in Santa Fe, New Mexico, 1894 Illustration by Charles Mente published in Harpers Weekly (Courtesy Fray Angelico Chavez Neg. No. 1-9b)

Stagecoach "Mountain Pride", Federal Plaxe, Santa Fe, New Mexico 1900 (Courtesy Muesum of New Mexico Neg. No. 010082)

John Potts Slough 1860 (Courtesy of Public Domain)

HIS TEMPER DID HIM IN
The Stormy Career Of John P. Slough

J ohn P. Slough, chief justice of the New Mexico Territorial Supreme Court in the late 1860s, might have enjoyed a distinguished judicial and military career had it not been for his quarrelsome and pugnacious nature, highlighted by temperamental outbursts accompanied by a profusion of profanity. His personality problems eventually led to a fatal encounter in a Santa Fe hotel.

A member of a prominent Ohio family, Slough was born in 1829 at Cincinnati and became a lawyer in his hometown. A Democrat, he was elected to the Ohio State Legislature at the age of 21 and was serving a second term in 1857 when he was expelled for knocking down one Republican legislator on the floor of the House and striking another with his fist.

Slough moved west to Kansas, where he had a brief but turbulent career as a Democratic candidate for various offices. In 1859, he joined the Pike's Peak gold rush to Colorado, where he practiced law in Denver and was chosen by miners as judge of the Colorado Territory Appellate Court.

At the outbreak of the Civil War in 1861, Colorado Governor William Gilpin appointed Slough commander of the First Colorado Volunteer Regiment with the rank of colonel. Slough had no military experience, even though his father had been a general, but he had been successful in recruiting Company A of the regiment.

Early in 1862, as a Confederate force from Texas was moving north through New Mexico towards Colorado and its gold fields, Slough led his Colorado regiment south into New Mexico in an effort to halt the Confederate advance. Moving down the Santa Fe Trail, the Coloradoans crossed over Raton Pass into New Mexico on March 9, 1862, and two days later joined the federal garrison at Fort Union, about 100 miles northeast of Santa Fe.

Despite military orders that he remain at Fort Union, Slough left the fort on March 22 with a force of about 1300 volunteers and regulars, and headed on down the trail towards Santa Fe, which was occupied by Texas troops. His command consisted of Colorado Volunteers, known as Pike's Peakers, and federal troops from Fort Union.

As the column moved towards Santa Fe, Slough began to fear for his own life, not because of the enemy below, but because of his own men. They were rugged miners and frontiersmen who disliked and mistrusted Slough, whom they regarded as an eastern aristocrat. Some even doubted his loyalty to the Union cause.

Slough's command met and clashed with the Texas troops on March 26 and 28 in Glorieta Pass, about 25 miles from Santa Fe. As the opposing force were battling on March 28, Major John M. Chivington, one of Slough's subordinates, led a force of 400 men that skirted around the battle lines and destroyed the Confederate supply train of about 70 wagons. Left high and dry with no supplies, the Texans began to retreat south out of New Mexico.

Although considered victorious at Glorieta, Slough resigned his military commission, angry because he was ordered not to advance into Santa Fe, and apparently fearing that he might be court-martialed for disobeying orders to remain at Fort Union. He headed at once to the nation's capital, where President Abraham Lincoln appointed him military commander of nearby Alexandria, Virginia, with a rank of brigadier general, a position he held until the end of the war despite various complaints against him.

Slough served as a pallbearer at President Lincoln's funeral, and Andrew Johnson, who succeeded Lincoln as president, appointed him chief justice of the New Mexico Territorial Supreme Court on January 26, 1866. He moved to Santa Fe with his wife and children and embarked upon his judicial duties, which included presiding at trials in various New Mexico communities.

Slough proved to be a good trial judge, although his strict efforts to bring decorum to territorial courtroom procedures that were notoriously lax and swayed by politics antagonized those who wished to maintain the status quo. He dismissed jurors without pay when they failed to reach verdicts, imprisoned or fined some jurors for misconduct, and set aside jury verdicts that he disagreed with. Slough also upset New Mexico tradition by ruling that Pueblo Indians were citizens of the United States, and that the long system of peonage, which included the holding of Indian slaves, was unconstitutional.

Off the bench, Slough campaigned for the erection of a monument in Santa Fe honoring Union soldiers who fell in New Mexico during the Civil War battles in the territory. His efforts were successful, and the New Mexico Territorial Legislature appropriated $1500 for the project in 1867 and appointed a committee to make the necessary arrangements and pick a site. The committee consisted of Slough, Herman H. Heath, the territorial secretary, and Felipe Delgado, the territorial treasurer.

View of the Plaza in Santa Fe, New Mexico. An obelisk, part of a monument to soldiers who fought against Native Americans is in the center of the Plaza. The Plaza, Santa Fe, New Mexico 1882 (Courtesy of Colorado Historical Society Call CHS.J1340)

The committee selected the center of the Santa Fe plaza as the site, and hired the firm of Michael McGee and Brother to erect a 32-foot high monument there. The dedication and laying of the cornerstone was conducted on October 24, 1867, with street processions and numerous speeches. Sealed inside the cornerstone were a variety of items, including coins, postage stamps, newspapers, names of civil and military officers in the territory, copies of territorial laws and even copies of the U.S. Constitution and Declaration of Independence.

The cornerstone was lowered into the ground at the conclusion of the ceremonies, but it was not until the following June that the monument was completed and set in place. The monument itself caused controversy for years to come, for it referred to Confederate soldiers as "rebels," honored New Mexico soldiers who fell fighting "savage Indians," and misspelled the second month of the year as "Febuary." (More than a century later, an unknown person obliterated the word "savage.")

Unfortunately, Slough did not live to see the completed monument, due principally to his frequent temper tantrums. For example, when a man employed by the military commissary in Santa Fe ordered Slough's young daughter out of the store for abusing his dog, Slough stormed into the commissary, shouted profanities at him and threatened to thrash him.

A Democrat, Slough played no leading role in partisan politics, but he often blamed partisan politics for his problems on and off the bench. When the New Mexico Legislature convened on December 2, 1867, the Republican majority selected Herman Heath, the Republican territorial secretary, to administer the oath, a privilege traditionally reserved for the chief justice. Slough considered this an insult, and blamed a number of Republicans for the slight including Heath and William F.M. Amy, former territorial secretary and acting governor.

Slough accosted Amy on a Santa Fe street that afternoon, grabbed him by the shoulders, accused him of plotting against him, and called him "a dirty dog and damned son of a bitch." Amy remained cool, but filed assault and battery charges against him.

Appearing in a local justice of the peace court the next after noon to answer the charges, Slough asked the judge if it was true that he had been bound over several weeks before to answer charges of perjury and malfeasance. When the judge admitted that it was true, Slough tore up the papers in his hand and strode out of the courtroom.

Heath then drew up a series of resolutions condemning Slough, which he planned to submit to the legislature, listing eleven specific charges against him and asking for his removal from office. The charges accused Slough of being "tyrannical, overbearing and frequently unjust" as a magistrate, that he intimidated juries, that he denounced territorial and military officials on the public streets of Santa Fe, and that he had frequently exhibited himself before the people under the direct influence of ardent spirits.

Agreeing to introduce the resolutions in the legislature, after another legislator had declined to do so, was William L. Rynerson, a newly elected Republican senator from Dona Ana County in southern New Mexico. Rynerson, a member of the Legislative Council, did not know Slough personally, although the two had similar careers.

Born in Kentucky in 1828, Rynerson walked to California following the 1849 gold rush, where he prospected for gold and studied law. He enlisted in the First California Infantry during the Civil War and was a sergeant with the California Column that marched overland to New Mexico in 1862, arriving after the Confederate retreat from the territory.

Rynerson was discharged with the rank of captain in 1866 at Mesilla, seat of Dona Ana County, at which time he had already purchased property in nearby Las Cruces and was involved in various mining and agricultural pursuits in the region. Slender, bearded, and standing well over six feet tall, he became referred to in political circles as "The Tall Sycamore of the Rio Grande."

The resolutions introduced by Rynerson in the legislature were passed by the Legislative Council on Saturday, December 14, 1867, and quickly caused a stir in Santa Fe. Late that afternoon, Slough entered the Exchange Hotel, also known as La Fonda, a one-story adobe structure opposite the southeast corner of the Santa Fe plaza. Entering the billiards room, he saw Rynerson playing billiards with an Army officer at one of the tables, and he sat down near the door about twenty feet from the two players. Slough remarked to some men sitting next to him:

> There is a strange combination, but one you frequently see in this world, a gentleman associating with a damned thief. I allude to that damned seven-foot son of a bitch playing billiards with Colonel Kinzie. He is a damned, lying thief and coward. He stole while he was in the army, and he has stolen since he got out of it, and he has stolen his present position, his seat in the legislature. I have denounced him as a damned son of a bitch, a thief and a coward, and the scoundrel doesn't have the courage to take it up.

Slough also suggested that Rynerson wear a collar inscribed "I am Heath's dog." Rynerson did not hear Slough's remarks, but was told about them. He went looking for the chief justice, but could not find him.

Early the next afternoon, Rynerson was standing by the fireplace in the hotel bar when Slough entered the door. Rynerson blocked his path and demanded that he retract what he had said about him.

"What did I say?" Slough asked.

"You called me a son of a bitch and a thief," Rynerson responded.

"I won't take it back," Slough replied.

"If you don't I will shoot you," Rynerson said, drawing a Colt revolver from his coat and aiming it at the chief justice.

"Shoot and be damned," Slough exclaimed, jerking his right hand from his vest pocket and causing a small Derringer pistol to fall to the floor. Rynerson fired at the same moment, the bullet piercing Slough's left side just above his hip. He fell to the floor, mortally wounded.

Three days later, on Wednesday, December 17, the *New Mexican* told of the fatal encounter under a headline reading "A Sad Occurrence." The article began:

> *On Sunday last a recontre took place in the Fonda in this city between Chief Justice Slough and Captain W.L. Rynerson, resulting in the mortal wounding of the former, who expired this morning. Captain Rynerson delivered himself up to the authorities, and is now under charge of Marshal (John) Pratt.*

As Rynerson was being escorted to jail, Slough's 10-year-old son slipped up behind him with a gun but was apprehended by guards before he could kill the man who killed his father.

Rynerson later stood trial on a murder charge but was acquitted on grounds of self-defense. The trial was held in March in Las Vegas, New Mexico.

Mrs. Slough and her children left Santa Fe and moved to her former home in Cincinnati. An insurance company refused to pay off her husband's $5,000 life insurance policy, due to the circumstances of his death, but she eventually won a settlement.

Rynerson served three terms in the legislature. During the 1870s, in addition to his varied farming and mining interests, he served as district attorney for the Third Judicial District, comprising Dona Ana, Lincoln and Grant counties. He married Mrs. Luciana Lemon, the widow of Republican leader John Lemon who was killed in the bloody Mesilla riot of 1871, and died in Las Cruces in 1893.

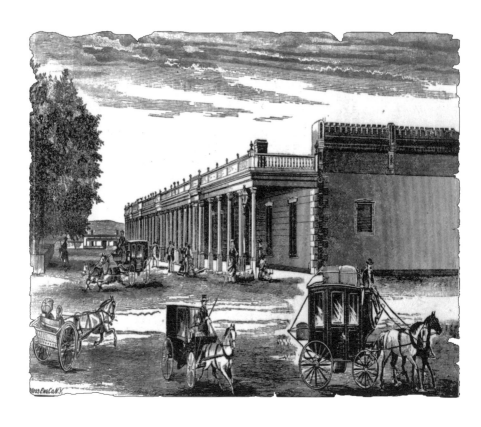

Palace of the Governors 1885 Illustration by William G. Ritch
(Courtesy Museum of New Mexico Neg. No. 011212)

ROBBERY OF THE SANTA FE DEPOSITORY
Conflicting Accounts Of The Crime

I t was no secret that the United States government had deposited $400,000 in cash in the U.S. Depository in Santa Fe. The Weekly New Mexican, on May 25, 1869, had published this account of the transaction:

> *The designated Depository in Santa Fe is again flush. Colonel Bridgeman, paymaster U.S.A., arrived from the States on Thursday last and delivered to the Depository in sealed packages four hundred thousand dollars in greenbacks, $300,000 of which we understand was placed to the credit of chief Paymaster Col. W.B. Rochester, and $100,000 to the credit of the United States treasury.*

The U.S. Depository in 1869 was located in the west room of the Palace of the Governors, where it was entrusted to the care of 69-year-old James L. Collins, a pioneer and prominent Santa Fe resident, who had held the position of depositary, or custodian, since 1866, and who occupied quarters in the palace. Collins, generally referred to as Colonel Collins due to his former rank with the New Mexico Volunteers, was scheduled to be replaced as custodian on Monday, June 7, 1869, by Captain E.W. Little.

But this was not to be. On Sunday morning, June 6, the day before Collins was to leave office, Santa Fe residents were startled by the news that the depository had been robbed of a large sum of money the night before and that Collins had been found shot to death in his office. The New Mexican reported on June 8:

The discovery was made by a servant girl who usually enters the colonel's room for the purpose of calling him to breakfast and making up his bed. The girl immediately announced the discovery to Mrs. James M. Edgar, daughter of Colonel Collins, who upon proceeding to the office and discovering the dead body of her father brought to the scene of the murder and robbery a number of gentlemen who had heard her lamentations.

Upon entering the room the diabolical work of the assassins and robbers was presented to view. The dead body of Colonel Collins lay upon the floor in a pool of coagulated blood with a pistol bullet hole through his heart, and over the floor were scattered various sealed packages of fractional currency and sundry piles of the same in small quantities, while the money vault and iron safe showed they had been broken open and all the bills of large denomination extracted and carried away. The amount of these it is believed is probably not less than $100,000.

An investigation indicated that robbers had forced open a back door of the building, used an iron bar to pry open the door of a small safe that held the key to the vault, and had used the key to open the vault. Awakened by the noise, the investigation concluded, Collins got up, lighted a candle, put on his slippers and walked through a hall to the office door, a revolver in his hand. It is believed that two quick shots were fired at him as he opened the door, one of the bullets piercing his heart.

Santa Fe citizens mourned the death of this pioneer. The *New Mexican* reported that Colonel Collins was one of the very oldest and most respected American citizens of New Mexico. He came to Santa Fe from Missouri around 1824.

Born in Crab Orchard, Kentucky, on February 1, 1800, Collins moved to Booneville, Missouri, at the age of nineteen, where he soon became interested in the Santa Fe trade. He made his first trip down the Santa Fe Trail to Santa Fe in 1826, transporting trade goods on pack animals. In 1828 he moved south to Chihuahua, Mexico, where he was engaged in the mercantile business until the outbreak of the Mexican War in 1846, when he moved back to Santa Fe.

Collins bought the Santa Fe *Republican* in the early 1850s, changed the name to the Santa Fe *Gazette*, and served periodically as editor of the weekly newspaper. He also served as superintendent of Indian Affairs in New Mexico from 1857 to 1863, and as a colonel with the New Mexico Volunteers during the Civil War.

Funeral services for Collins were held June 8 at the Santa Fe home of his son-in-law, James N. Edgar. "The procession thence to the Masonic cemetery in the northern part of the city was a large one," the New Mexican reported, "composed of the military, federal and territorial officers, carriages with families and citizens generally."

On the day of the funeral, $65,500 of the money missing from the depository was found in an old brewery north of town, or, according to another account, in a privy at an abandoned house owned by J.M. Edgar, who, according to earlier accounts in the newspapers, also owned the brewery. It was believed that $33,000 was still missing.

Strangely enough, Santa Fe newspapers then fell silent about the crime, one of them noting that the cause of justice would not be served by repeating stories and rumors about the unfortunate affair. There is evidence, however, that the silence was observed to protect the reputation of an esteemed citizen.

What may have been the truth about the crime was revealed in 1897 by Louis C. "Sandy" Wardwell of Albuquerque, a pioneer stagecoach driver who published his recollections in a series of articles appearing in the Albuquerque *Weekly* News. Wardwell wrote that he was employed as a driver for Col. Collins in 1869 and hauled ore from the mines at San Pedro, south of Santa Fe, in which Collins had an interest. Here is his account of what happened:

I drove for about two months, and then went into Santa Fe for supplies, and the Colonel's son-in-law, Edgar, sent me down to La Vajada (Bajada) where he had a ranch. When I got back to Santa Fe the next morning the Colonel was dead -- had committed suicide. He had hid out about $75,000 in an out house and the old brewery. He had scattered all the money around the floor and shot himself through the head -- sacrificed himself to give his daughter a stake, and Edgar, his son-in-law, did not have the nerve to keep it and gave it all away, and the good old man died in vain.

Officially, the crime was never solved. Collins is now buried in Santa Fe's National Cemetery, his remains moved there when the Masonic and Odd Fellows' Cemetery was abandoned.

La Bajada (the descent), Santa Fe, New Mexico (Courtesy Muesum of New Mexico Neg. No. 135196)

The Murdered Government Official at Santa Fe.

From the Cincinnati Times, June 7.

Hon. JAMES L. COLLINS, United States Designated Depositary at Santa Fé, New-Mexico, was shot through the heart on the night of the 5th of June, and the Depository robbed of $100,000. Hon. JAMES L. COLLINS was a man of marked personal bravery, and passed through the Mexican war and the war of the rebellion with the commendation of all who knew him. He was of marked assistance to Colonel DONIPHAN, who reached General TAYLOR after the battle of Buena Vista with his Missouri volunteers. The frontier experience of Colonel COLLINS was of great utility to the Indian service—for he was Superintendent of Indian Affairs when that office was separated from the Executive of the Territory of New-Mexico in 1856. He was designated Depositary, June, 1866.

The New York Times

Published: June 10, 1869

James L. Collins newspaper story published June 10, 1869 (Courtesy The New York Times)

Lt. Colonel John R. Baylor (Courtesy of Public Domain)

CONFEDERATE OCCUPATION OF SANTA FE

Leave Behind Empty Champagne Bottles

An account of the Confederate occupation of Santa Fe in 1862 was published in the Santa Fe Weekly Gazette on April 26, 1862, the day the newspaper resumed publication after having been closed down for more than a month by the invading army from Texas. The occupation of New Mexico's capital began on March 10 when a small group of Texans made their appearance in the city, the Gazette reported, adding:

> *They were Texans in name but in reality they were men who had formerly lived here and had gone to Mesilla to join the enemy. They were followed on Thursday (March 13) by about seventy more under the command of Major (Charles L.) Pyron. These, who in all numbered about eighty men, constituted the Texan strength in Santa Fe for the space of ten days when they were joined by the balance of Maj. Pyron's command, which increased their numbers by about two hundred.*

The Confederate invasion of New Mexico had started in July, 1861, when several hundred Texas troops, under the command of Lieutenant Colonel John R. Baylor, had occupied the southern New Mexico town of Mesilla and captured the Union garrison at nearby Fort Fillmore. Baylor proclaimed the southern third of New Mexico, south of the 34th parallel, as the Confederate Territory of Arizona, with Mesilla as its capital, and himself as governor.

A major campaign to conquer all of New Mexico for the Confederacy began in February, 1862, when the Sibley Brigade, about 2500 Texas troops under the command of General Henry Hopkins Sibley, began moving north up the Rio Grande Valley towards Albuquerque and Santa Fe. Union forces at Fort Craig, about twenty-five miles south of Socorro, failed to halt the Confederate advance at the February 21 Battle of Valverde, and the Sibley Brigade continued north to occupy Albuquerque on March 2.

Santa Fe, indefensible and expecting the imminent arrival of Texas troops, began making hasty preparations for the Confederate occupation of the city. New Mexico Governor Henry Connelly and members of his staff abandoned their offices in the Palace of the Governors and fled east about sixty-five miles up the Santa Fe Trail to Las Vegas, New Mexico, where they established a temporary capital.

On March 3, the *Gazette* reported, Major James L. Donaldson, Union quartermaster at Santa Fe, dispatched a train of 108 wagons loaded with military provisions to Fort Union, about 100 miles up the Santa Fe Trail. Some provisions that could not be shipped were distributed the following day to Santa Fe citizens or destroyed. All that was left for the invading Texans, the newspaper said, were two large hay racks that stood in the government corral behind the Palace of the Governers. The hay could not be burned without endangering the city.

According to the newspaper, Colonel James L. Collins, New Mexico superintendent of Indian affairs, concealed in "a skillful manner" all good intended for distribution to Indians, and although the Texans searched long and diligently for the Indian stores, they failed to find them until March 31 when they were beginning their retreat from the city.

John T. Russell, editor of the *Gazette*, surrendered the keys to the newspaper office on March 22 in compliance with a hand-delivered order signed by Major Pyron. The next day, General Sibley, who was still in Albuquerque, issued a proclamation promising amnesty to all

New Mexico citizens and militiamen who would lay down their arms, return to their homes and pursue their respective avocations.

Major Pyron's command left Santa Fe on March 25 and began moving up the Santa Fe Trail with the goal of capturing Fort Union, unaware that they were on a collision course with a large body of Colorado Volunteers who had reached Fort Union and were approaching Santa Fe. The Texans clashed with the vanguard of the Colorado troops on March 26 near the mouth of Apache Canyon, about twenty-five miles from Santa Fe, after which the Union force retreated back through Glorieta Pass.

Confederate troops commanded by Colonel William R. Scurry, which had been camped at the village of Galisteo south of Santa Fe, joined Pyron's command, and the combined Confederate force moved through Glorieta Pass and battled the main body of Colorado troops on March 28 at Alexander (Pigeon) Valle's ranch, a major stopping place on the Santa Fe Trail. Leading the Pike's Peakers, as the Coloradoans were known, was Colonel John P Slough.

While that battle was in progress, a Colorado detachment led by Colonel John M. Chivington circled through the mountains and destroyed the Confederate wagon train that was parked behind the Texas lines. The Texans, having lost all their supplies, had no choice but to retreat. They began arriving in Santa Fe on Saturday, March 29. The *Gazette* reported:

> *They began arriving here in the afternoon in squads of different sizes and continued to come in until a late hour Sunday morning. Their appearance clearly manifested the severe usage to which they had been subjected. Some rode, some walked, and some hobbled in. All were in a most destitute condition in regard to the most common necessities of life.*

Thomas Green was a Texas landowner, politician, and soldier who served as a brigadier general in the Confederate Army during the American Civil War. He was considered as one of the finest cavalry leaders in the Trans-Mississippi Theater 1814-1864(Courtesy Public Domain)

An exchange of prisoners was negotiated on March 31, the newspaper said, during which two prominent Santa Fe citizens, J.M. Gallegos and Facundo Pino, were released after having been arrested by the Texans and confined for the duration of their occupation of the city.

Colonel Thomas Green's regiment of from 500 to 600 Texans arrived in Santa Fe on April 4, the newspaper continued, and the entire Confederate force abandoned Santa Fe on April 7 and 8 and retreated south towards Albuquerque, ending the occupation of the city.

"Some citizens who had made common cause with them whilst they were in the city went with them and we assume will accompany them to Texas," the *Gazette* said. They included William Pelham, former surveyor general.

The newspaper said that the Texans appropriated large amounts of clothing and other supplies from Santa Fe merchants before leaving, and that General Sibley had issued an order for the seizure of all funds in the territorial treasury "and the money appropriated to either the General's own private use or for some other purpose."

The *Gazette* referred to the March 28 engagement at Alexander Valle's ranch as the Battle of Valley's Ranch, but noted that Colonel Scurry called it the Battle of Glorieta. History adopted Scurry's designation. The newspaper said:

> *Governor Connelly is again established in the Palace. While he was absent some of the Texas officers occupied the venerable building but none of them attempted to exercise the functions of Governor. The only memento they left behind for our worthy Chief Magistrate were some of Sibley's proclamations and empty champagne bottles.*

Left behind when the Texans retreated south were at least one hundred of their number who were too sick or wounded to travel. While recuperating, those who cared for them included a number of prominent Santa Fe women, including the wife of General E.R.S. Canby, Union commander in New Mexico. It was not until late August that the last of them were escorted south to Fort Bliss, Texas.

Also left behind by the retreating Texans, although it was not known at the time, were twelve large cannon barrels that were buried at night at a still secret location.

Col. Richard Harison Weightman, C.S.A. (1816-1861) First Territorial Delegate to Congress from New Mexico 1851-1853 (Courtesy Museum of New Mexico Neg. No. 50516)

SOME SANTA FE DUELS
They Were Not Always Fatal

Weightman-Houghton

Richard H. Weightman, a 31-year-old Maryland native and Mexican War veteran, had been practicing law in Santa Fe for only a short time in 1849 when he began feuding with Joab Houghton, chief justice of the New Mexico Territorial Supreme Court. Judge Houghton, a 38-year-old New York native, had arrived in Santa Fe in 1843 as a civil engineer and merchant, and although having only a slight knowledge of the law, was appointed chief justice in 1846 by General Stephen Watts Kearny when American troops occupied the city.

Weightman and Houghton were leaders of rival factions on the question as to whether New Mexico should be admitted to the union as a state or as a territory and whether or not Texas had valid claims to the region. Weightman launched a series of verbal and written attacks against Houghton, accusing him of fraud and misconduct in connection with his judicial duties. Houghton responded with the following letter to Weightman, dated September 9, 1849:

> *Sir: In consequence of slanderous words used by you in conversation with Lieutenant Taylor at the Sutler's store in Albuquerque, with J.L Hubbell, Esq., at Socorro, at Santa Fe, and generally throughout the Territory, within the last few weeks, I demand of you an unequivocal retraction of such slanders, or the satisfaction due from one gentleman to another. (Signed) J. Houghton.*

Weightman responded to the challenge in a letter to John H. Quinn, an attorney in Judge Houghton's court, dated September 19, 1849, which concluded with the words: "I accept his challenge, and will meet him this day at as early an hour as can conveniently be agreed upon between yourself and the gentleman who will hand this to you."

The two antagonists, accompanied by their seconds, met in an arroyo at the north edge of Santa Fe, behind the present-day Scottish Rite Cathedral, and each was handed a pistol. At the command to fire, Weightman alone fired, but missed. Houghton, who was a bit deaf, ducked his head as the bullet whizzed by his ear and shouted, "I didn't hear the command to fire."

Weightman held his hands up and said, "All right. You have the right to shoot. Fire now."

At that moment, the seconds rushed in and urged Weightman to apologize to the judge so that the rest of the duel could be called off.

"I'll apologize as far as being sorry is concerned," the attorney said, "but I can't take back what I said, judge, for it is so."

Houghton accepted this as an apology and both men walked away.

View of San Francisco Street in Santa Fe, New Mexico 1882. Men stand on wooden sidewalks and the dirt street. (Courtesy Denver Public Library Call No. Z-4118)

Beck-Gorman

A deadly sidewalk duel with Bowie knives stunned Santa Fe residents on March 26, 1858. The principals were Preston Beck Jr., of the mercantile firm of Beck and Johnson; and John Gorman, a clerk in the nearby store of Richard Owens. Both stores faced the Santa Fe plaza.

Beck, a 38-year-old bachelor, had arrived in Santa Fe from Missouri in 1845 and had amassed a small fortune in a mercantile business that extended to all parts of the territory. His character and popularity were summed up by the Santa Fe Weekly Gazette with these words:

> *Mr. Beck's correct business habits, courteous and high-toned bearing, and manly and generous qualities of head and heart, have won him an esteem and confidence rarely enjoyed by any man.*

Francisco Griego, a young man who was employed by Beck at the mercantile store, was walking past the Owens store on the evening of March 25, 1858, when Gorman called him into the store and began questioning him about Griego's sister-in-law, who was Gorman's girlfriend. Gorman accused Griego of taking the woman to several dances, and when Griego hesitated to answer, Gorman picked up a stick and began clubbing him about the head, face and shoulders. He then threw the bleeding young man out into the street.

Word of Griego's severe beating reached Beck the next morning, the *Gazette* reported, and he walked at once to the Owens store, accosted Gorman in the doorway, and denounced him for beating his employee. Gorman denied the beating at first, but as the argument became more heated, he drew a knife and advanced toward Beck "threatening to serve him as his servant had been served." Beck, who was standing outside the door, drew his knife, and the newspaper, on March 27, published this description of the duel:

Each commenced parrying the motions of the other, when Gorman made a sudden strike, thrusting his knife into Mr. Beck's abdomen near the navel. As quick as a thought the lick was returned, Mr. Beck's knife penetrating to the hilt the left side of Gorman in the region of the heart.

Each held to his knife. Mr. Gorman made several quick licks which were skillfully wended off by Mr. Beck, without hitting Gorman, when the latter fell upon his back, his arms outstretched, and expired.

As Gorman fell to the sidewalk, Beck picked up his overcoat, threw it over his shoulders, walked back to his store and then to his room, walking firmly while holding his hand over his wound. Dr. J.H. Sloan was sent to dress Beck's wound. When he arrived, Beck asked him to go treat Gorman first, but the physician declined to go, not informing Beck that Gorman was dead.

Beck's condition deteriorated during the days that followed, and he was advised to get his affairs in order. Needing help to treat his patient, Dr. Sloan asked that an express rider be sent to Albuquerque to obtain the services of Dr. David C. DeLeon, an Army surgeon.

Undertaking this mission of mercy was Albert Pfeiffer of Santa Fe, a native of the Netherlands who later was to achieve a measure of fame as a colonel with the New Mexico Volunteers during the Civil War and Indian campaigns in New Mexico.

Riding horseback, Pfeiffer left Santa Fe late on the morning of April 5, 1858, rode the seventy miles to Albuquerque in five hours and fifty minutes, and returned to Santa Fe with Dr. DeLeon the next morning, completing the round-trip in twenty-two hours.

The valiant effort was in vain, however, as Beck died at his home on April 8 after nearly two weeks of suffering. His only survivors were his father in Missouri and a brother in California.

Illustration from Harper's Monthly Magazine of a gambling saloon in Santa Fe, New Mexico 1854 (Courtesy Museum of New Mexico Neg. No. 014963)

Smith-Stinson

Two professional gamblers, Van C. Smith and Joe Stinson, spent the afternoon of June 20, 1876, drinking in Stinson's saloon on San Francisco Street near the Santa Fe plaza. Both men were considered quiet, respectable citizens when sober, but hell-raisers when they got drunk, and they got pretty drunk that afternoon.

Smith, a 39-year-old native of Vermont, had a long and varied career in New Mexico and Arizona as a rancher, lawman, prospector, Army scout and gambler. He and a partner, Aaron 0. Wilburn, had established a small community in southeast New Mexico in 1869 that Smith named Roswell in honor of his father, Roswell Smith of Omaha, Nebraska.

Stinson, a native of Maine, had arrived in New Mexico in the late 1860s, and in 1871 he and a partner, William H. "Little Billy" Baker, were co-owners of a saloon with gambling tables in the new mining community of Elizabethtown in northeast New Mexico. Years later, some of Baker's recollections of Simpson were published in the Albuquerque *Daily Citizen* on June 9, 1903. Baker was living in Denver at the time.

"He was a big, good natured fellow when he was sober, but he was a bad man when he got his load on," Baker recalled. "He didn't pick any trouble, but he was awful ready for it when he thought it was up to him." Like the time in 1871 when Wall "Shot-in-the-Eye" Henderson, a desperado described by Baker as "a marksman who had laid out several pretty confident fellows," reportedly by shooting them in the left eye, stormed into the Elizabethtown saloon, took it over, and invited everybody up to the bar for free drinks.

"You may think you own this place," Henderson told Stinson and Baker, "But I'm running it for the time being."

Stinson, dealing faro at a card table, ignored him, and let him have his way. Eventually, however, his patience began to wear thin.

"I'll kill you sometime," Henderson told Simpson.

"All right, but don't let me catch you at it, Wally," Simpson replied.

A few hours later, when Henderson and Simpson came face:to face, Henderson reached for his gun.

"That's all he did," Baker recalled. "Before he could get it out, Joe had three holes in him and he was flat on the floor, down and out." Also dead.

Stinson calmly reached for a bottle, telling Baker, "It's a pity, but one of us had to live."

Why Stinson and Smith got into a heated argument in the Santa Fe saloon that Tuesday afternoon in 1876 is unknown, but it got to the point where Stinson challenged Smith to meet him at the Soldiers Monument in the center of the Santa Fe plaza and fight it out with pistols. Smith accepted the challenge, and both men left to obtain weapons.

Stinson, having armed himself with a Colt navy revolver, walked to the plaza and stood at the east side of the monument waiting for his opponent to appear. Smith soon appeared, walking to the plaza from the east, and Stinson noticed to his dismay and anger that Smith was carrying a Winchester repeating rifle. The plaza was surrounded by a low picket fence, and as Smith was opening the east gate, Stinson, without any warning, drew his pistol and started firing at him.

Two bullets grazed Smith in the right hand and right hip, another shattered a fence paling by the gate, and a fourth sailed across the street and through the window shutters of the Fisher and Lucas jewelry store, frightening one of the owners who was working at a table by the front window.

Smith managed to get off two shots with his rifle, but the bullets went high, one striking the granite shaft high on the northeast corner of the monument, and the other glancing off the southeast corner.

Downtown pedestrians, startled by the gunfire, went to the aid of Smith, taking him to the Broad Gauge Saloon where a doctor treated his minor wounds. Stinson walked leisurely across the west side of the plaza and entered a drug store.

When both men had sobered up the next morning, they expressed regret over the incident, and agreed to be friends. Smith said he didn't recollect anything about pistols being specified for the duel.

The Santa Fe *New Mexican*, in its report of the duel, suggested that future belligerents settle their differences "on top of Mount Baldy where nobody would be endangered by stray bullets," adding:

> *Both gentlemen are known to be quiet, peaceful citizens, endowed with as much of that article termed 'clear grit' as usually falls to the share of Western men; and what astonishes their friends is the fact that such men could plan and carry out so desperate engagement in the very heart of the city, whether drunk or sober, where the lives of so many disinterested persons were endangered.*

Buffalo at water hole John D. Howland 1900 (Courtesy Colorado Historical Society Call No. CHS-X3146)

A PIONEER SANTA FE ARTIST
The Adventurous J.D. Howland

John Dare "Jack" Howland, best known today for his early paintings of Western wildlife, was living in Santa Fe in the early 1870s and working as a portrait artist when he decided to embark on a new adventure in his already eventful life. The son of an Ohio riverboat captain, he envisioned an artistic voyage for hundreds of miles down the scenic but shallow and sometimes treacherous Rio Grande.

Howland's adventurous life in the Rocky Mountain West had started at an early age. Born in Zanesville, Ohio, on May 7, 1843, he was a grandson of that city's founders and a direct descendant of John Howland, who had arrived in the New World on the Mayflower in 1620. He ran away from home at age fourteen and made his way west to St. Louis, where he joined American Fur Company voyages up the Missouri River.

After trading with Indians at various fur company posts, and taking part in buffalo hunts, he headed for the Pike's Peak gold camps in Colorado where he panned for gold without much success. He joined the Colorado Volunteers at the beginning of the Civil War and accompanied them south into New Mexico in 1862 where they halted the Confederate advance at the Battle of Glorieta.

Howland continued his military service as a captain of scouts during the Indian wars and provided campaign sketches for *Harper's Weekly* and Frank Leslie's *Illustrated Newspaper*. Following his military service, he went abroad and studied art in Paris for two years. Later, he served as secretary to the Indian Peace Commission, which attempted to negotiate treaties between the U.S. government and Plains Indian Tribes from 1867 to 1869.

Howland was living in Santa Fe as early as 1872, for records show that he paid $34 to Santa Fe's Exchange Hotel for his April board that year. The Weekly New Mexican, which referred to the artist as Captain Jack Howland, noted early in 1874 that he was a Santa Fe portrait artist and was displaying his work at a local photography gallery owned by photographer H.T. Heister.

While in Santa Fe, the newspaper noted, Howland had painted portraits of such prominent New Mexico citizens as Major Lawrence G. Murphy and Colonel Emil Fritz of Lincoln County; the Abraham Staab family of Santa Fe; Dr. Samuel Russell, New Mexico Indian agent, and Louis Clark, a prominent merchant of Alcalde north of Santa Fe. (Clark was shot to death in Alcalde in 1876.)

It was in July of 1874 that Howland and Heister decided to leave Santa Fe and embark on a river journey down the Rio Grande to Mesilla, in southern New Mexico, painting pictures and taking photographs along the way. No such river journey, it was said, had ever been taken.

A boat was built, probably a large raft, of which no description was given by the newspapers, other than it was of four tons burden and was called the McGuffin. Howland and Heister hauled it by wagon south to Santo Domingo Pueblo, where the road south from Santa Fe reached the Rio Grande.

A detailed description of the river journey was published by the Mesilla *News* in September, 1874, when the artist and photographer reached their destination. The article said:

> On the 6th of August the 'McGuffin' with a cargo of 4,000 pounds consisting primarily of artists materials and provisions, including a camera for taking stereoscopic views, was pushed out from the rocky bank at Santo Domingo, and our bold adventurers trusted their fortunes to the swift current of the Rio Grande.

The sailing was easy the first day, the article continued, and the two men reached Bernalillo that night after passing San Felipe Pueblo and Algodones. Their first difficulties were encountered between Bernalillo and Albuquerque, where they found the river to be quite wide and shallow. Sometimes they had to get out into the water and pry their boat over sand bars.

Arriving in Albuquerque, they decided to lighten the boat by removing a portion of the heavy cargo and shipping it south by wagon. They spent four days in Albuquerque accomplishing this task.

Embarking from Albuquerque with their lightened load, Howland and Heister sailed leisurely on down the river, the newspaper continued, stopping occasionally to sketch or photograph such villages as Pajarito, Isleta Pueblo, Peralta, Los Lunas, Tome, Belen, La Joya, Polvadera, Socorro and San Marcial. Sailing around Valverde Mesa, they soon reached Fort Craig.

"Here our adventurers were the recipients of that generous hospitality for which the gallant officers of the 15th Infantry are proverbial," the newspaper said. "They were the guests of Major Whittemore and his fair lady, of whose kindness they speak in the highest terms."

Officers at Fort Craig warned the two visitors of the river dangers ahead, including "a gloomy canyon filled with cataracts, falls and rapids" as the two men boarded their craft. Continuing south, the boat with its two-man crew passed the village of Paraje and soon plunged into "a great canyon where the pent-up waters rushed and foamed," the article said. Sometimes the boat took on a few gallons of water as it navigated dangerous rapids, some of them descending eight or ten feet in less than one hundred yards through the rock-filled passage. There were ten such rapids in a thirty-mile stretch.

"And so they floated on where never white man has sailed before," the newspaper continued, "down by Alamosa, past McRae, beneath Elephant Rock (now Elephant Butte), and under the shadow of Castillo (Cuchillo?) Negro, down by Palomas and San Jose and Santa Barbara; as evening closed they passed the ruins of old Fort Thorn, long since abandoned."

With the last obstacle passed, the article continued, the McGuffin now sailed triumphantly past Fort Selden, Leasburg, Picacho, Dona Ana and Las Cruces, pulling up at Mesilla on September 5. The river voyage had lasted about a month, but no more than twenty days of this was consumed in actual traveling.

John Dare Howland was back in Santa Fe two years later, the *New Mexican* now referring to him as Major Jack Howland. The newspaper reported on October 10, 1876, that Howland was in Santa Fe on his way to the Centennial Exposition in Philadelphia, where some of his artwork was on display.

Since leaving Mesilla, Howland said, he had tramped over a large part of Texas and Mexico before settling in the city of Chihuahua, Mexico, where he purchased an interest in a silver mine and worked as a portrait artist.

He apparently was back in Santa Fe a year later, for the New Mexican reported on April 24, 1877, that Major Howland was in charge of the Soldier Cemetery (now the National Cemetery.)

Howland settled in Denver, Colorado, in 1878, where he resumed his career as a Western artist. He married Esther Mary Talmadge of New York in 1884, after which he returned to Paris for advanced art study. He founded the Denver Art Club in 1886, and was credited with designing the Civil War monument at the Colorado State Capitol. He died in Denver in 1914.

Maternal Solitude, landscape painting with cattle and coyotes John Dare Howland 1848
(Courtesy Colorado Historical Society Call No. CHS-X3017)

Lamy family mausoleum at the Rosario Cemetary,
Santa Fe, New Mexico Photo by Gregory Lucero

A SANTA FE SCANDAL
Archbishop's Nephew Accused Of Murder

John B. Lamy was a 29-year-old bachelor in 1870 when he left his home in France and settled in Santa Fe. His move probably was at the invitation of his French-born uncle, Bishop Jean Baptiste Lamy of Santa Fe, and came five years before his uncle was elevated to archbishop.

John (originally Jean) Lamy, said to have been his uncle's namesake, used the anglicized version of his given name in Santa Fe, possibly to avoid confusing him with his prominent uncle. Santa Fe newspapers periodically and mistakenly referred to him as John B. Lamy, Jr. He was said to have been a man of limited means, but of an honest, prudent and industrious nature.

His fortunes improved when he met and married the beautiful and vivacious Dona Mercedes Chaves of Santa Fe, a young lady of wealth and high social standing in the city. She was well educated, having received her education at the Visitation Convent at Georgetown, outside Washington, D.C.

Born in the village of Las Padillas near Albuquerque in 1853, Dona Mercedes Chaves de Lamy had the distinction of being the daughter of one New Mexico governor, Jose Chaves; the granddaughter of another, Francisco Xavier Chaves; and the niece of two others, Mariano Chaves and General Manuel Armijo, all serving during the period of Mexican rule, 1821-1846.

The newlyweds moved into an elaborately furnished home that Mrs. Lamy owned on San Francisco Street, a short distance west of the new St. Francis Cathedral that was nearing completion. In 1876 the couple embarked on a year-long tour of Europe, visiting most of the capital cities.

The marriage appeared to be a happy one, although Lamy preferred a quiet home life to social activities, while his wife preferred lively company in society circles.

Their lives began to change late in 1878 when Francis Mallet, a young and handsome French architect, arrived in Santa Fe at the invitation of Archbishop Lamy to help correct and perfect the design of the new cathedral. As the *New Mexican* at Santa Fe reported:

> *He was a man of very prepossessing appearance, with a flow of brilliant language, and was a fine conversationalist. Being also a Frenchman, he naturally fell in with (John) Lamy, and between the two there soon sprung up an intimate friendship.*

Mallet spent many evenings with Mr. and Mrs. Lamy at their residence, and the three were often seen riding about town in the Lamy's horse-drawn carriage.

"In this manner things ran on till April," the newspaper reported in 1879, "when rumors began to circulate that Mr. and Mrs. Lamy had had trouble, and that Mr. Mallet was visiting their home more frequently than propriety tolerated."

Lamy blamed Mallet for his wife's growing discontent, and told her that the architect was no longer welcome in their home. She replied that it was her home, and that she could invite anybody that she pleased. She left the house in May, 1879, stayed with friends and filed for divorce, accusing her husband of cruel and inhumane treatment. She also asked for restoration of her property.

When she failed to get a divorce in July, as she had expected, as no property settlement had been reached, her husband offered to take her back, but she refused. Periodically, she and Mallet were seen walking together in the outskirts of Santa Fe.

Lamy, according to the Santa Fe newspaper, began to deteriorate physically and mentally, working himself into "a condition of frenzy." The tragic result of his condition was told in the Weekly *New Mexican* on Saturday, September 6, 1879: "Last Monday afternoon, about 5 o'clock, Francis Mallet, while standing in the door of the Exchange Hotel, was shot dead from behind by John B. Lamy Jr,"

Mallet had just arrived at the hotel, which stood opposite the southeast corner of the Santa Fe plaza, and was looking out over the plaza from a doorway when Lamy, grasping a pistol in both hands, approached him from behind, placed the gun at the back of Mallet's head, and fired.

"Mallet stood erect for a few seconds, then fell heavily backwards on the floor, and died without a word or struggle," the *New Mexican* reported.

Lamy fled across the street and into a saloon, the article added, then emerged and gave himself up to two police officers. Mrs. Lamy, upon hearing of the tragedy, attempted suicide by drinking a small bottle of aconite, but survived through the efforts of Dr. Robert W. Longwill.

It was not until a year later that Lamy stood trial in Santa Fe on the murder charge. On September 23, 1880, the jury returned a court-instructed verdict of not guilty by reason of temporary insanity.

The Lamys reconciled and lived together for many years in their Santa Fe home. As the years went by, most Santa Fe residents were unaware of the tragic events in the couple's early lives.

John B. Lamy died on May 21, 1928, at the age of 86; and his wife, Mercedes Chaves de Lamy, followed him in death on February 20, 1931, at the age of 77. Today, their remains are in wall crypts in the small Lamy Mausoleum in Santa Fe's Rosario Cemetery, along with the remains of Mrs. Lamy's mother, Dona Manuela Armijo de Chaves, wife of Governor Jose Chaves, who was 63 when she died in 1876.

President Rugherford Hayes and Lucy Hayes on their wedding day, December 30, 1852
(Courtesy Public Domain)

PRESIDENT HAYES ENJOYS SANTA FE
General Sherman Doesn't Like It

A twenty-one gun salute at Fort Marcy (then in the center of town) awakened Santa Fe citizens from their slumbers early on the crisp autumn morning of October 28, 1880, the cannon booms reverberating through the narrow streets of the centuries-old New Mexico capital. The cannonading inaugurated a day of celebration, a day eagerly anticipated for weeks, a day to welcome and entertain important visitors from the nation's capital. Headlines in the Santa Fe *Daily Democrat* that evening echoed the excitement: "HAIL! ALL HAIL! To our Chief Magistrate, Rutherford B. Hayes. The Only President Who Ever Visited Santa Fe."

During its two hundred and seventy year history under the flags of Spain, Mexico, the United States, and briefly, the Confederate States, Santa Fe had never been visited by the current ruler of any country. When Ulysses S. Grant visited Santa Fe in July, several months before President Hayes arrived, the ex-president was welcomed as "the first of all men who, having held the high office of chief executive of any nation, has ever set foot upon the soil of New Mexico."

Santa Fe had taken on a gala, holiday appearance for this presidential visit. Places of business were decorated with flags, streamers and bunting. Early risers began converging on the center of town in horse-drawn carriages, preparing to form a procession to the depot to meet the special train carrying the president and his party, which was scheduled to arrive at nine o'clock. The U.S. Ninth Cavalry band assembled and began playing martial and patriotic airs, the music punctuated by the continuing sounds of cannon fire.

Hayes, winding up a four-year term as president, was homeward bound from a rail tour of the western states and territories, even though the itinerary of the return trip was still fraught with frontier danger. The president, along with members of his family and staff, had traveled to California by a northern rail route and was returning east by the southern route, which included a gap of more than one hundred miles between as yet unfinished rail lines in southwest New Mexico, requiring a dangerous journey by horse-drawn vehicles through a barren region frequented by Apache raiding parties.

From California, the presidential party had headed east across southern Arizona on the Southern Pacific Railroad line to the end of the track, a camp just designated as Lordsburg. Here, early on the morning of October 25, the travelers disembarked from the train and were greeted by a military escort consisting of men of the Ninth Cavalry and Fifteenth Infantry, equipped with military ambulances with which to transport the visitors on the next and most rugged and dangerous leg of their journey.

Those boarding the military vehicles included President Hayes; his wife, Lucy Webb Hayes, known as "Lemonade Lucy" for her stand against serving alcoholic beverages in the White House; their twenty-two year old son, Rutherford Platt Hayes; General of the Army William Tecumseh Sherman and his daughter, Rachel Sherman; Secretary of War Alexander Ramsey; General Alexander McDowell McCook, and Mrs. J.C. Audenried.

Although danger on the overland route had diminished considerably with word that the Apache chief Victorio had been killed and most of his band wiped out by Mexican troops in Chihuahua a little over a week earlier on October 14, General Edward Hatch, commander of the U.S. Military District in New Mexico, had taken special precautions to speed the presidential party through Apache domain and protect them from attack. In addition to the military escort that accompanied the carriages, military relay stations had been established at intervals along the route, temporary camps with tents, provisions, and fresh horses for the vehicles.

From rail's end, the visitors were escorted east along the old Butter-field Trail to Fort Cummings, an isolated and recently re-activated military post, surrounded by a high adobe wall, at the mouth of Cooke's Canyon. Here the weary travelers spent a restful night after a fifteen-hour trip covering sixty miles.

Leaving the fort the next morning, the visitors were escorted north-east to the village of Las Palomas, on the west bank of the Rio Grande near present-day Truth or Consequences, where they camped for the night at some hot springs. Fording the river the next morning at Fest's Crossing, near the southern edge of present-day Elephant Butte Reservoir, they were transported east to Round Mountain, a camp at track's end of the Atchison, Topeka and Santa Fe Railroad, then building south for an eventual link with the eastward pushing Southern Pacific line.

At this point they were able to resume their journey by rail. Hayes and his companions traveled north through Socorro and Albuquerque and arrived late that night at Galisteo Junction (present-day Lamy), a main line station from which a branch rail line led sixteen miles north to Santa Fe. The travelers spent the night on the train at Galisteo Junction, a special train consisting of two Palace Pullman cars and a baggage car.

A great many of the 6600 Santa Fe residents were gathered at the Santa Fe depot the next morning to greet the incoming train carrying the presidential party, including United States Marshal John Sherman Jr. nephew of General Sherman. The train, due at nine o'clock, and nearly an hour late, was greeted with cheers and band music as it approached the depot. Those disembarking, in addition to those previously mentioned, included Mr. and Mrs. J.W. Herron, Colonel and Mrs. Barr, Dr. David L. Huntington, Colonel John W. James, Mrs. J.G. Mitchell and Colonel John W. Jameson, all otherwise unidentified by the Santa Fe newspapers.

The visitors were escorted to waiting carriages, and a procession was formed, led by the Ninth Cavalry band, which proceeded through the streets to the central plaza. Here the guests of honor left their carriages and assembled on the roofed bandstand on the plaza.

William G. Ritch, Photo by George C. Bennett 1880 (Courtesy Museum of New Mexico Neg. No. 010759)

Placita at the home of Territorial Secretary and Acting Governor W. G. Ritch, Santa Fe, New Mexico, 1885 (Courtesy Museum of New Mexico Neg. No. 055013)

Welcoming the guests on behalf of the Territory of New Mexico was William G. Ritch, acting governor in the absence of Governor Lew Wallace, who had gone home to Indiana to vote in the November presidential elections. His welcoming address, and the speeches given by the visiting dignitaries, were published in full that day and next by the Santa Fe *Daily Democrat*. His remarks included the following welcome:

> *We welcome you to these mountains, to this historical plateau upon the high line of the continent, and to this antique and most ancient of all the capital cities of the land, and to its freedom and hospitality. That you and your party have deemed it important to include the southern territories in your trans-continental tour, subjecting yourself to toils of the journey and the perils that beset the pathway, in order to visit and learn the necessities of our people, and view in person the land and its wealth of empire, is certainly very assuring.*

The acting governor asked the president to call the attention of Congress to various New Mexico problems, including the need for public schools, the settling of defective land titles, and better protection from nomadic Indian marauders.

At the conclusion of his talk, Rich introduced President Hayes to the large crowd that filled the plaza. The president's short address was informal and non-political. A Republican, he was not seeking re-election to a second term, and even if he were, citizens of United States territories were not eligible to vote in presidential elections. He stated:

> *I am very glad to meet this large assemblage of people of New Mexico and of Santa Fe. In the short conversation which I shall have with you, very desultory and scattering in its treatment of the topics that have been suggested, I shall not attempt, at large, to talk upon any particular subject.*

We have been traveling - - it will be two months next Sunday - - traveling, perhaps up to this time, eight thousand miles, meeting everywhere assemblages of American citizens and talking to them always, I believe, in every case with myself and the gentlemen who are with me, in natural, off-hand talk, believing they are much more satisfactory on the whole than prepared addresses, even if we had opportunities to prepare addresses.

The president, who like Sherman and McCook had been Union generals during the Civil War, went on to stress a common love of American union, liberty and the flag, causing one man in the crowd to ask a companion, "Is he referring to the stars and stripes?"

The president's concluding remarks:

Santa Fe, I believe, is claimed to be by intelligent people here to be the oldest town, that it was settled before St. Augustine, before our forefathers found Plymouth Rock, or the cavaliers settled in Virginia.

Now, my friends, you will, when your railroads are completed, get every advantage that your location gives you; the splendid scenery that surrounds you, these snow-capped mountains with their historic associations, will draw the traveler that crosses the continent; almost the last man will visit you. The next thing to a good home, as the traveler knows, is a good hotel, and I learn that you are constructing one, and among these faces I have no doubt there is a man who knows how to keep a good hotel.

I must not talk too long. We have a number of gentlemen with us, not only good talkers, but who, I have a suspicion, like to talk. Secretary Ramsey generally never likes to talk, but when he starts to go anywhere he gets there, and when he starts to talk he will say something sooner or later. I have heard your voices and you have heard mine. I bid you good morning.

The president was loudly applauded at the close of his speech, and the Ninth Cavalry band played "Hail Columbia." The acting governor then introduced Secretary of War Alexander Ramsey, whose informal talk brought frequent laughter from the crowd:

> *My friends and fellow citizens, Santa Fe and New Mexico have always been to me, from my earliest youth, a most mysterious and interesting country. I have often dreamt that I thought I would like to see them, that I would like to come up and see you in your mountain home. At length I am here and congratulate myself upon it.*
>
> *I have wished to be born in a Spanish clime, it is an easy way of acquiring the Spanish language. But I was born on the banks of the Susquehanna, and never got beyond the Pennsylvania Dutch.*

All that New Mexico lacked, Ramsey continued, was sufficient water, and that he would not be surprised to learn that some "ingenious Yankee" had inaugurated an Imperial Consolidated Water Manufacturing Company. He said that New Mexico had vast mineral resources that were not yet known or developed, and that eventually they would bring prosperity to the region.

> *In other regions that have developed like resources, they were not known until they struck them. Michigan was claimed to be such a barren, worthless field that it would not pay for a survey of it. That was the opinion of the surveyor general of Ohio, but I do not blame anybody from Ohio for that.*

The crowd laughed, realizing that the good-natured barb was aimed at his traveling companions, Hayes, Sherman and McCook, all Ohio natives. He concluded his talk by predicting that New Mexico's vast mineral resources would bring prosperity to the region.

The next and final speaker was General Sherman, chief of the nation's military forces, whose dislike of New Mexico was equaled only by his dislike of politicians and newspaper reporters. On more than one occasion he had suggested that the United States go to war with Mexico again to make her take back New Mexico.

Sherman had the reputation of being "frequently reckless in speech," and his long and rambling talk, filled with derogatory remarks about native New Mexicans and their lifestyles, was a prime example. Some excerpts from his speech:

> *Fellow citizens of Santa Fe, I have been here before, and come to you as a friend again. I have experienced your hospitality, and have known some of your race of Mexicans who seem to be passing away and replaced by a stronger, more vigorous and determined people. Those who remain and still possess the land will be protected in their rights and property, as far as the law can protect them, but they themselves must learn that they must bring their lands to a higher state of cultivation, or take place in the ranks of the past.*

> *You must improve your land and develop the vast resources of your country, or a new race will come in here and displace you. I hope and pray that the next time I come here I shall surely find the old race of Mexicans that we found here long ago in the past improved, brought to a higher degree of improvement and cultivation.*

Sherman, speaking six years before Geronimo's surrender brought Apache warfare to an end, defended continuing military operations in New Mexico.

You need not sit and growl and grumble at General Hatch and his soldiers, I know that they have done all that was possible. General Hatch and his soldiers will stand by you, but you must protect yourselves and not expect everything of them.

You all know here in New Mexico when the Indians are pursued by our troops they scatter through the hills, and you might as well try to catch rattlesnakes and lizards, that they make resistance too great for the troops and citizens to overcome.

I am glad that Victorio is dead, and wish he had been killed by our troops, but that was not possible. He was driven over the line by our troops, when the Mexican troops ran him down and killed him.

Two years ago I went out among the Navajos and called them about me and talked to them, as I am talking to you now. I had not, at the time, a man with me; that is, I had no escort, no soldiers to protect me, and I believe if you let them alone they will never trouble anyone again. If you establish whiskey shops among their number and sell them aguardiente, deal out vile whiskey to them, it is a different matter.

I have seen bigger rows in this town than I ever saw in the Navajo country. I remember one when a man was killed in a saloon over there (pointing across the plaza) whose name was . . .

"Aubry," shouted several pioneers in the crowd who remembered the 1854 episode when Francis X. Aubry was stabbed to death in the Mercure Brothers saloon. Acknowledging the crowd, Sherman resumed:

Yes, Aubry. You used to have nothing but rows in this town, but now it looks like a Sunday school town. You must not expect to spend your time in idleness, you have got to work for your-selves. We will keep some troops here and keep it safe to settle here, but you have got to do your share of fighting if there is any fighting to be done.

You must improve your land, and make the most of the re-sources that your location affords you, and get rid of your burros and goats. I hope ten years hence there won't be any adobe houses in the territory. I want to see you learn to make them of brick, with slanting roofs. Yankees don't like flat roofs, nor roofs of dirt.

While Santa Fe newspapers reported that the other speeches were followed by applause and cheers, no such reception was noted for Sherman's speech.

"General Sherman put his foot in it today as usual," the Democrat noted that evening, adding that the newspaper later would publish some comments on his speech that would not be of a complimentary nature. The newspaper reported on October 30:

A great many of our citizens are very bitter against General Sherman for the derogatory manner in which he referred to the Mexican population. It hardly became him as a guest of our citizens, a great many of the better class of whom are Mexicans, to criticize them so harshly. His scurrilous association of the native Mexican being of a lower class than the Yankee will not advance the interest of the Republican party, of which he is a shining light, at least it certainly will not in New Mexico.

Following the speeches on the plaza, President and Mrs. Hayes were escorted to the home of Lehman Spiegelberg, a prominent Santa Fe merchant, where they met and shook hands with groups of school children. Later, they were guests at the Palace Avenue home of L. Bradford Prince, chief justice of the New Mexico Supreme Court, where it became evident that they did not share Sherman's opinion of adobe houses with flat roofs.

The Daily *New Mexican* reported that Judge Prince showed his guests his New Mexico library and Indian relics, and that the president "was highly delighted with the cozy and cheerful appearance of the interior of the house and of its pleasant arrangement with the rooms opening upon the *placita.*" The newspaper added that "Mrs. Hayes was equally charmed with the comfortable appearance of an adobe residence, and said that if they ever built a new house it should be of this material."

A public reception for Hayes, Sherman and Ramsey was held that evening in the Palace of the Governors during which the visitors shook hands with hundreds of Santa Fe residents. During the reception, the plaza in front of the historic building was brightly illuminated with bonfires and calcium lights, while the Ninth Cavalry band performed on the bandstand. Following the reception, the presidential party boarded the special train at midnight to resume their journey to the nation's capital.

9th Cavalry Band on plaza, Santa Fe, New Mexico, 1880 (Courtesy Muesum of New Mexico Neg. No. 050887)

SANTA FE DAILY DEMOCRAT.

SANTA FE, N. M., THURSDAY EVENING, OCTOBER 23, 1880.

y & Co.

HAIL! ALL HAIL!

To our Chief Magistrate, Ruth-erford B. Hayes,

The Only President Who Ever Visited Santa Fe.

Address of Welcome by Gov. W. G. Ritch.

THE PRESIDENT'S REPLY.

In honor of the reception of Presi-dent R. B. Hayes the ancient city put on holiday attire, and each street strove to show our honored president its full patriotism by display of flags banting and streamers. Passing up San Francisco street from the Surve-yor General's office. All the stores and places of business were decorated with the stars and stripes. The Grand Central Hotel, Democrat office, Ilfeld, Spiegelberg's, Second National Bank, and on the plaza, Z. Ztaab's were ar-rayed in bunting and flags. From ear-ly in the morning until eleven o'clock, cannonading music and general rejoi-cing seemed to be the unanimous or-der of our city. The reception of the President and party will occur at 7:30 o'clock P. M. at the Palace, to which no invitatios have been issued, but everybody cordially invited to attend.

Address of welcome by Governor Ritch:

The honor and pleasure has been deputed to me to welcome you to New Mexico and to its capitol.

The first chief magistrate of the Re-public either to visit the great south-west, or to take this Territory en route across the continent, our people are specially gratified with the opportu-nity to extend to your Excellency, to Hon. Secretary Ramsey, to the Gen-eral of the Army, the ladies and gen-tlemen accompanying, and to each a hearty, cordial, and sincere welcome. (Great Cheers.)

We welcome you all among a liber-ty and union-loving people represent-ing not only the descendents of the intrepid Latin explorers of this conti-nent in the first century of European emigration, but likewise of the genial energy and enterprise, and irresistable pluck and push of our day and genera-tion, hailing from every state of the Union and from every civilization of the universe. (Applause.)

We welcome you to these moun-tains, to this historical plateau upon the high line of the continent, to the antique and most ancient of all the capital cities of the land, and to its freedom and hospitality. (Great and prolonged applause.

We welcome you as the chief mag-istrate of this great nation during a pe riod historic in its sound finances, its honesty and equity in administration, conspicuous in the revival of trade and

and immediate protection of our peo-ple and frontier from the maraudings and horrors of nomadic savagery that have been only so recently a very pro-sent reality.

And now we again say to you, Presi-dent Hayes and party, to the distinguished party accompanying you. Welcome

Fellow Citizens:—I now have the pleasure of introducing to you, Ruth-erford B. Hayes, President of the Uni-ted States. (Great and continued ap-plause and cheers for President Hayes)

Mr. Chairman of the Committee, La-dies and Gentlemen:

I am very glad to meet this large assemblage of the people of New Mexico, and of Santa Fe. In the short conversation which I shall have with you, very desultory and scatter-ing in its treatment of the topics that have been suggested, I shall not at-tempt, at large, to talk upon any par-ticular subject. We have been travel-ing(it will be two months next Sunday) traveling, perhaps, up to this time, eight thousand miles; meeting every-where assemblages of American cit-izens and talking to them always—I believe, in every case with myself and the gentlemen who are with me, nat-ural off-hand talk—believing that they are much more satisfactory on the whole than prepared addresses, even it we had opportunities to prepare ad-dresses. We are met everywhere with the same cordial feeling, not because, I think, of anything achieved by us, not because of anything in our char-acter or our history deserving such attention, but because we find, as we believe, there is a common love of American union and love of American liberty, secured by American institu-tions; and, therefore, the people are disposed to treat with respect those who, for the time being, happen to be the representatives of that union and and its institutions. (Applause.) I was glad to hear from the Chairman of the Committee, the phrase applied to this people, though composite they are composed of different nationalities, the phrase li-berty-loving and union-loving; not that it was necessary that we should hear it in order to know it. That old mo-nument, it is not very old, but when the monument tells the story, we know all the United States know that the people of New Mexico, under some-what trying circumstances, in days that tried mens souls, was indeed, and they are union loving and liberty-loving (Great applause) Wherever such peo-ple are I may assure you, fellow citi-zens, I feel very much at home. (Great applause) In our journey we have frequently been to places where, as perhaps you have observed, they have taken pains to tell us that they

railroads are completed, get every ad-vantage that your location gives you the splendid scenery that surrounds you, these snow capped mountains with their historic associations will draw the traveler that crosses the con-tinent ; almost the last man will visit you. The next thing to a good home, as the traveler knows, is a good hotel, and I learn you are constructing one, and among these faces I have no doubt there is a man that knows how to keep a good hotel. With the prob-able early connection between the road from the west and from the east, your own line of great travel will con-nect you with the great line of the world, from London to Canada, from New York to San Francisco, and it will be for you to get your share of the good things passing along that line.

I must not talk too long; we have a number of gentlemen with us, not only good talkers but who, I have a suspicion, like to talk. (Laughter.) The former Governor of Minnesota, Gov. Ramsey, generally never likes to talk, and you can hardly get him to talk ; but when he starts to go anywhere he gets there, and when he starts to talk he will say something sooner or later, (Laughter.) I have heard your voices and you have heard mine a good deal; I bid you good morning.

(The President was loudly applaud ed at the close of his speech, and the band played "Hail Columbia.")

THE recent election in Indiana took the majority of the Democratic party by surprise, but it was only another plain case of cause and effect; the no-mination of Franklin Landers being the cause; his defeat the effect. The Democracy of Indiana have always been too willingly and anxious to pan-der to the Greenbackers; these two parties can never affiliate; their aims differ too widely and had the Demo-cracy nominated for governor a man who could have polled the full vote of of his party, no sane man can say that they would not have been successful; therefore the recent election can have no bearing whatever on the Presiden-tial contest. Our nominee for that high office is one for whom no demo-crat will hesitate to cast his vote, and many Republicans, likewise, who see that a further continuance in power of the present men, of whom James A. Garfield is the most illustrious, and of whose principal and theories of govern-ment he is the ablest exponent, would be detrimental to the interests of our country. Instead, therefore, of our recent reverses hurting the

FA

NEW I

THE PLAZA

Fine Wines,

L

Free Lunc

Neat, Cle

EN (

KI

The Pla

Unquestionably

Three T

BO

EER WEEK (
PER WEEK (

JO

L. SP

BU

Portion of Santa Fe Daily Democrat, Thursday, October 23, 1880 Headline: "Hail! All Hail!" President Hayes visit. (Courtesy of author's collection))

Maj. Gen. William T. Sherman, in May 1865, Portrait by Mathew Brad (Courtesy Public Domain)

Lew Wallace Portrait (Courtesy of authors collection.)

THE GOVERNOR AND THE OUTLAW
Lew Wallace And Billy The Kid

L ew Wallace believed that his distinguished career entitled him to a better appointment than the one offered to him in 1878 as governor of the distant and turbulent Territory of New Mexico at a salary of $2400 a year. From his home in Crawfordsville, Indiana, about fifty miles northwest of Indianapolis, he pondered the offer from the Rutherford B. Hayes Administration in the nation's capital.

The son of a former Indiana governor, the 51-year-old Wallace was a talented lawyer, writer and artist with an impressive military background. He had served as a second lieutenant during the Mexican War, and had risen to the rank of major general with an Indiana regiment during the Civil War. He had served as an officer on the court martial that convicted the Lincoln assassination conspirators, and was president of the commission that convicted Confederate Captain Henry Wirz of mistreating and killing Union prisoners at the prison camp at Andersonville, Georgia. He also spoke Spanish, having learned the language in Mexico while aiding the revolutionary forces of Benito Juarez against Maximilian, the puppet emperor of Mexico.

Although he had been hoping for a more prestigious appointment, Wallace apparently decided that serving as governor of New Mexico would give him time to complete a lengthy novel he was writing and an opportunity to invest in some of the territory's booming gold and silver mining claims. After some deliberation, he accepted the appointment.

Leaving his Indiana home on September 25, 1878, Wallace traveled by rail to Trinidad, Colorado, which was as far west as the tracks of the Atchison, Topeka and Santa Fe Railroad had reached at the time. From here, he traveled the remaining 185 miles to Santa Fe by buckboard, with an overnight stop at Cimarron, New Mexico, where he was the guest of lawyers Frank W. Springer and William D. Lee. Upon reaching Santa Fe, he told of the hardships of the bone-jarring buckboard journey in a letter to his wife, Susan B. Wallace:

> *I reached here about 9 o'clock on the night of the 29th of September, having ridden on a buckboard from Trinidad. When the vehicle drew up in front of the hotel in this town, I took a look at it when I jumped, or rather crawled off it at the door of the Fonda here. I was thankful beyond expression, in truth I do not believe you could have stood it all – you would have been sick in every bone, dead in every muscle.*

Wallace went on to call the buckboard "an instrument of torture," describing it as "a low-wheeled affair, floored with slats; the springs are under the seats and so weak that with the least jolt they smite together with a horrible blow, which is all the worst if overloaded, as was the case when I rode on them."

After spending the night in the hotel, Wallace walked across the Santa Fe plaza to the Palace of the Governors to inform Governor Samuel B. Axtell that he had been suspended from office and that he had come to replace him. Although Axtell, like Wallace, was a Republican, the Republican Administration had removed him from office due to complaints that he had been ineffective in solving civil conflicts that

El Palacio, Santa Fé. (From Pencil Sketch by Gen. Wallace.)

Pencil sketch by General Wallace of "El Palacio" Palace of the Governors, Santa Fe, New Mexico 1885 (Courtesy Mueseum of New Mexico Neg. No. 143221)

had been raging in both Colfax and Lincoln counties, resulting in a breakdown of law and order, and that he had sided with some of the warring factions.

Wallace was sworn in as governor that afternoon, and soon established his office and residence in the rambling, adobe structure that he referred to as the Old Palace. He soon turned his attention to the civil violence that had been raging for months in Lincoln County in southeast New Mexico. Sparked by a feud between two mercantile firms, the Lincoln County War had escalated into bloody warfare between rival economic and political factions and their outlaw allies that included a series of ambush and revenge slayings.

In an effort to bring the violence to a halt, Wallace issued an amnesty proclamation on November 13, 1878, granting a general pardon for misdemeanors and offenses committed in Lincoln County against territorial laws from February 1, 1878, to the date of the proclamation. This proclamation brought a measure of peace to Lincoln County for several months. The pardon, however, did not include those already under indictment in connection with the offenses.

Early in February, 1879, Wallace journeyed by buckboard back to rail's end at Trinidad, Colorado, to meet his wife, Susan, and their 25-year-old son, Henry L. Wallace, who had traveled by rail from Indiana. The three traveled to Santa Fe by buckboard, which Susan, as had her husband before, described as "an instrument of torture."

Meanwhile, violence was brewing anew in Lincoln County, erupting once again on February 18, 1879, when Huston Chapman, a lawyer representing a member of one of the opposing factions, was shot and killed by members of the other faction while standing unarmed on a street in Lincoln, the county seat. The renewed violence prompted Wallace to make his first visit to Lincoln County, arriving there on March 5 with a military escort.

While there, Wallace received a hand-delivered letter, signed William H. Bonney, saying that he was present when the lawyer was killed, that he knew who did it, and that he was willing to testify against them if it was in the governor's power to annul indictments pending against him. "I am called Kid Antrim," he concluded, "but Antrim is my step-father's name."

The young letter writer, eventually known as Billy the Kid, was hiding out in the nearby village of San Patricio at the time. He was not included in Wallace's amnesty proclamation, for as a leading member of one of the opposing factions, he had been indicted for his part in the 1878 ambush slaying of Lincoln County Sheriff William Brady.

Wallace responded with a hand-delivered letter asking him to come alone to the Lincoln home of Squire Wilson on the night of March 17, adding: "I have authority to exempt you from prosecution if you will testify to what you say you know."

Cautiously, the Kid arrived at the house on schedule, holding a revolver in one hand and a rifle in the other. During their secret meeting, Wallace asked the Kid to testify as to what he knew about the killing of the lawyer, promising that "in return for you doing this, I will let you go scot-free with a pardon in your pocket for all your misdeeds."

Old courthouse where Billy the Kid was tried, Messilla, New Mexico (Courtesy Muesum of New Mexico Neg. No. 057238)

When the Kid expressed concern that his testimony could put his life in danger, arrangements were made for him to submit to a mock arrest with incarceration in an empty room at the Lincoln residence of Juan B. Patron. He submitted to the false arrest and jailing on March 23.

The popularity of the young prisoner surprised the governor.

"A precious specimen named 'The Kid,' whom the sheriff is holding here in the Plaza, as it is called, is an object of tender regard," Wallace wrote to Washington. "I heard singing and music the other night; going to the door, I found the minstrels of the village actually serenading the fellow in his prison."

The Kid testified before the Lincoln County grand jury in April and secured indictments against Billy Campbell, Jesse Evans and James Dolan, whom he identified as being responsible for the lawyer's death. Campbell and Evans had disappeared into Texas, however, and Dolan escaped conviction.

Wallace was surprised that the grand jury had returned more than 200 indictments against about 50 defendants in a county with a voting population of only 150. To his dismay, most escaped conviction by disappearing or taking advantage of the amnesty proclamation. Both Wallace and the Kid testified at a May court of inquiry that investigated the role of military officers in the civil warfare.

Meanwhile, challenging the governor's authority to grant immunity to anyone in connection with the Lincoln County War was William L. Rynerson, district attorney in neighboring Dona Ana County and a supporter of one of the warring factions. He pursued murder charges against the Kid for his part in the 1878 ambush slaying of Sheriff William Brady and had the case transferred to Dona Ana County, where the Kid had but few friends.

Wallace, frustrated and discouraged after spending weeks in Lincoln County, returned to his Santa Fe office in May, apparently willing to forget Lincoln County problems and the pardon he had promised William Bonney. It may have been at this time that he wrote, "Every calculation based on experience elsewhere fails in New Mexico."

For the Kid, Wallace's apparent betrayal was to have far-reaching consequences. Still hearing no word on an official pardon from the governor, and knowing that Rynerson was determined to convict him, he left his pretended place of confinement in Lincoln on June 17, 1879, mounted a horse, and rode off into New Mexico's eastern plains.

Back in Santa Fe, Wallace was happy to leave the Lincoln County problems behind and now felt free to follow pursuits more to his liking. Sometimes accompanied by his wife or son, he traveled to mountain regions in northern and southern New Mexico, examining and investing in mining properties. During the evenings, he worked until midnight in his bedroom behind the executive office in the old palace completing the manuscript of his lengthy biblical novel, entitled *Ben-Hur: A Story. Of the Christ.*

Wallace also inaugurated plans for restoration work on the centuries-old and deteriorating palace. In addition, he worked to preserve the old Spanish archives that his wife and he found piled in boxes and barrels and scattered on the floor of an abandoned palace outbuilding.

In February, 1880, The Atchison, Topeka and Santa Fe Railroad was completed south through New Mexico from Colorado to Santa Fe, continuing south toward the Mexican border. Wallace, happy that

General Lew Wallace in study, Crawfordsville, Indiana (Courtesy Museum of New Mexico Neg. No. 040340)

his buckboard-riding days were over, helped drive the last rail spikes in Santa Fe along with General Edward Hatch, New Mexico military commander, and L. Bradford Prince, New Mexico chief justice.

Wallace completed the manuscript of *Ben-Hur* in the summer of 1880. Published on November 12 of that year by Harper and Brothers in New York, the book became a best seller. Susan Wallace, also a writer of considerable ability, published six books during her lifetime, including *The Land of the Pueblos*, consisting of her New Mexico experiences and impressions. That book, published in 1888 by John B. Alden of New York, contained pen and ink illustrations by her husband.

Needless to say, Wallace was not pleased when a rather sensational editorial in a New Mexico newspaper late in 1880 brought William Bonney back to the governor's attention. The Las Vegas *Gazette*, on December 3, 1880, claimed that an outlaw gang of forty or fifty hard characters was harassing stockmen in the Pecos River Valley of New Mexico and the Texas Panhandle and terrorizing people of Fort Sumner and other New Mexico communities.

The editorial claimed that the gang was under the leadership of "Billy the Kid," marking the first time that Bonney was referred to in print by that designation, and that other members of the gang included Charlie Bowdre and Dave Rudabaugh. The newspaper also reported that James Carlyle, a resident of White Oaks in Lincoln County, had been shot down by Billy the Kid.

Billy the Kid, as he was known from then on, wrote a letter to Wallace in Santa Fe, dated Fort Sumner, December 12, 1880, denying the newspaper's accusations that he was the leader of an outlaw gang, writing that "there is no such organization in existence."

"I have been at Sumner since I left Lincoln making my living gambling," he added, probably stretching the truth as there was evidence that he and some of his friends had been stealing and selling ranch livestock, a rather common practice at the time. He also denied that he had shot down Carlyle, writing that in a brief exchange of gunfire Carlyle was accidentally killed by one of his own men, which probably was the truth.

Pat Garrett (1850-1908), Las Vegas, New Mexico
(Courtesy of Public Domain)

The governor, obviously unimpressed by the Kid's letter, responded by posting a reward notice reading: "Notice is hereby given that five hundred dollars will be paid for the delivery of Bonney, alias "The Kid," to the sheriff of Lincoln County.

Less than two weeks later, on December 23, 1880, Pat Garrett, sheriff-elect of Lincoln County, led a posse that captured the Kid and three of his friends at an abandoned rock house at Stinking Springs, east of Fort Sumner. Charlie Bowdre was killed in the process, and taken into custody were the Kid, Dave Rudabaugh, Billy Wilson and Tom Pickett.

The prisoners were first taken north to Las Vegas, and then to Santa Fe by rail, arriving in Santa Fe on the evening of December 27. They were placed in the Santa Fe jail on Water Street, a few blocks southwest of the Santa Fe plaza and the governor's residence. When Garrett visited the Santa Fe jail the next day, he learned that his prisoners had not eaten, and that the food that had been sent to them from a nearby hotel was eaten by the jailers.

On January 1, 1881, the Kid wrote a short note to Wallace, reading: "I would like to see you for a few minutes if you can spare the time," and signed William H, Bonney. The governor was not at his residence a few blocks away, however, as he had left for the East Coast a week before and was not due back for several weeks.

Jailers discovered on February 28 that the Kid and three companions were close to digging •their way out of the jail, having almost completed an escape tunnel and concealing the dirt and rocks in their mattresses. The Kid was shackled and placed in solitary confinement.

During March, the Kid wrote three more letters to the governor, asking for his help, and all of them went unanswered. The hand-delivered letters said in part:

> *March 2: I wish you would come down to the jail to see me. It will be in your interest to come see me.*

> *March 4: I expect you have forgotten what you promised me this month two years ago, but I have not. I have done everything that I promised you I would but you have done nothing that you promised me.*

> *March 27: Dear Sir, for the last time I ask, will you keep your promise? I start below tomorrow. Send answer by bearer.* The Kid was removed from the Santa Fe jail the next day and transported by train south to Dona Ana County to stand trial for his part in the ambush slaying of Sheriff Brady. Tried before a jury in Mesilla, the county seat, he was convicted of murder on April 9 and sentenced to death by hanging, the execution to take place in Lincoln on May 13, 1881.

Wallace, meanwhile, was busy winding up his affairs as governor of New Mexico. On March 9, 1881, he submitted his resignation in a letter to newly-elected President James Garfield, who accepted it and appointed Lionel A. Sheldon as his successor.

Wallace was still in Santa Fe on April 28, 1881, when Billy the Kid escaped from custody in Lincoln by killing his two guards, J.W. Bell and Robert Olinger, then riding off on horseback. Two days later,

Wallace published a reward notice reading: "Billy the Kid. $500 Reward. I will pay $500 reward to any person or persons who will capture William Bonny, alias The Kid, and deliver him to any sheriff of New Mexico. Satisfactory proofs of identity will be required. Lew Wallace, Governor of New Mexico."

According to a newspaper article published years later, Wallace reacted to the Kid's escape by keeping a loaded revolver close at hand at all times and using it each morning to practice his marksmanship skills. "Brave as Governor Wallace had shown himself to be, he recognized his danger and prepared to meet it," began an article in the Albuquerque *Daily Citizen* on December 14, 1893. The article went on to say:

From the day upon which Billy the Kid escaped from the Lincoln County jail, a close observer entering the (governor's) office might have detected lying on the table, partially hidden among papers and scraps of manuscript, the glint of a pistol, for the governor was never without one while he knew that his arch-enemy was at large.

The people of Santa Fe were well aware that the head of the territorial government was preparing for war, for every morning about 7 o'clock the sharp crack of a revolver being fired resounded from the corral in the rear of the gubernatorial residence. It soon became known that it was Governor Wallace improving himself as a pistol shot preparatory to an impromptu duel with Billy the Kid.

A figure had been marked on the adobe wall of the corral and the governor filled it full of holes. He became so expert that he could knock an imaginary eye out of the figure at 20 paces. He made no bones of the matter, and, in fact, could be easily seen from the adjoining houses.

Maxwell house and Officers Quarters, Fort Sumner, New Mexico where Billy the Kid was shot by Pat Garrett 1870 (Courtesy Muesum of New Mexico Neg. No. 045559)

If Wallace thought he had anything to fear from transient Billy the Kid, these fears vanished on May 30, 1881, when he boarded a •train for a trip east and a new assignment as minister to Turkey.

Before leaving Santa Fe, Wallace shipped a carload of New Mexico souvenirs by railroad freight to some of his friends in Indiana. Among the items was a burro, the Spanish word for a small donkey, which he thought would make a pet for the children of a former neighbor. Later, the railroad freight office in Albuquerque received the following telegram from an Indiana freight office: "Car No. 27390, Albuquerque, consigned to Wallace, arrived minus one bureau, plus one jackass. Please trace and advise."

It was six weeks after Wallace left New Mexico that 21-year-old William Bonney, alias Billy the Kid, whose true name was Henry McCarty, was shot and killed by Sheriff Garrett at Fort Sumner on the night of July 14, 1881. Garrett collected the $500 reward, and with the help of a ghostwriter, published an unauthentic book titled *The Authentic Life of Billy the Kid.*

Wallace, unknowingly, had helped to create a legendary figure of the young outlaw by failing to pardon him for his misdeeds, ignoring his requests for help, and offering rewards for his capture. With the promised pardon in his pocket, the Kid probably would not have been convicted of murder and sentenced to hang, would not have made a dramatic escape from custody by killing his two guards, and would not have been tracked down and killed for the reward money. In short, there would be no outlaw folk-hero known as "Billy the Kid."

William H. Bonney ("Billy the Kid") New Mexico 1878
(Courtesy of Public Domain

THE GANG

Top Left: Tom Pickett (Courtesy Museum of New Mexico Neg No. 89720) Top Right: Dave Rudabaugh (Courtesy of Public Domain) Bottom Left: Charles Bowdre and wife Mannela Herrera Bowdre Photo by James N. Furlong 1878 (Courtesy Museum of New Mexico Neg. No. 105048)

Cochise, Apache Chief (Courtesy Museum of New Mexico Neg. No. 133930)

COCHISE MEETS THE PRESS
Apache Chief Interviewed In Southern New Mexico

Cochise, the renowned Chiricahua Apache chief, was nearing the end of his long and militant career late in 1871 when he arrived at the Southern Apache agency at Canada Alamosa (the present-day village of Monticello) in south central New Mexico and announced that he wanted to settle down and live at peace under agency supervision, as most of his people had been killed off in warfare. Accompanying him from their traditional stomping grounds in southeastern Arizona were more than two hundred men, women and children of his band.

His sudden appearance on September 28, 1871, caused a flurry of excitement among agency officials and villagers alike. News that Cochise wanted to live at peace at the new Apache agency was greeted with skepticism by many residents of southern New Mexico. Some suspected treachery, and some expressed doubt that the Apache at Canada Alamosa was the celebrated chief.

Deciding to go see for himself was Nehemiah Bennett, editor of *The Borderer*, a Las Cruces weekly newspaper. Before embarking on a one-hundred-mile horseback ride north to Canada Alamosa, the editor decided to take with him somebody who could positively identify Cochise. He chose Charles Coleman of Las Cruces, who had known Cochise ten years before while working as a blacksmith at a stagecoach station at Apache Pass, Arizona.

Mounting Texas mustangs, Bennett and Coleman left Las Cruces on October 24, 1871, and a three-day trail ride north up the Jornada del Muerto brought them to Fort McRae, a military post a short distance east of the Rio Grande near the present-day town of Truth or

Consequences. Here they met Orlando F. Piper, the Indian agent at Canada Alamosa, and accompanied him about thirty miles northwest up the Alamosa River to the Apache agency.

Piper expressed doubt that Cochise would talk to the newspaperman, but agreed to lead the two Las Cruces visitors to his camp on Cuchillo Negro Creek, about a dozen miles south of Canada Alamosa. The three left the agency on October 29.

Bennett, in his later newspaper article, described the difficult trip on horseback on a narrow trail that took them over Cuchillo Mountain to the isolated Apache camp. They went unarmed and passed several Apaches on the steep trail. Upon their arrival at the camp they were met by Loco, a Mimbres Apache chief, who directed them to the lodge occupied by Cochise, on a high point overlooking the camp.

"Loco, A Chief of the Warm Spring Apaches" (Courtesy Museum of New Mexico Neg. No. 076905)

"Cochise was lying in his lodge as we rode up but came out as soon as he heard the voice of the agent and greeted him with a shake of the hand and a deep, guttural 'bueno," Bennett wrote.

Coleman asked Cochise if he remembered him. The chief examined him closely and replied, "Yes, Charlie, Apache Pass, much time ago, put shoes on mules." Also greeting Coleman were Cochise's wife, Dos-teh-seh, daughter of the late Apache chief Mangas Coloradas, and several of the older Apache warriors.

A blanket was spread under a cedar tree, and the visitors sat down with Cochise, Loco and Cheever, the latter a Coyotero Apache chief who had recently arrived at Canada Alamosa with nearly two hundred members of his band. Cochise offered his guests some *tiswin*, an Apache corn liquor, and agreed to make some comments for the newspaper.

"Tell the people I have come here to make peace, a good peace," he told Bennett. "Tell them I like this country and wish to spend the remainder of my life here at peace with all men, that I do not want to leave this place and go anywhere else."

Cochise added that the whites were to blame for his going on the warpath, and that many lies had been told about him. He admitted that he had done some "bad things," but said he was not responsible for all the bad things attributed to him.

Asked if his warriors were going to learn to be farmers, Cochise replied that "the Apaches were not made to work, the Great Spirit had not given them heads to learn, that it was so long to planting time that should he talk to his young men about it now they would get a pain in their heads thinking about it and perhaps die."

Asked about his age, Cochise replied that if he had been a farmer, and noticed the times of planting and harvesting, he would have known how many seasons he had lived, but that an Apache never took notice of the seasons.

"We should suppose him to be about 50 years old," Bennett wrote, "but it would puzzle the best judge to decide if he was that or several years older or younger."

This is the way Bennett described Cochise:

He is a tall and finely formed man, and except for the long and deep furrows across his forehead, gives very little indication of age. His hair is intensely black, his face smooth and slightly ornamented with yellow ochre.

His mouth is splendidly formed and flexible, his nose prominent, and his eye expresses no ferocity. The whole expression of his countenance is pleasant, and one looks in vain for a gleam of that ferocity which has so long been attributed to him. A sense of melancholy and thoughtfulness is clearly discernable in his features while in conversation, and his voice is full, clear and heavy.

Bennett's account of his visit with Cochise occupied more than a page of *The Borderer* on November 1, 1871, with headlines reading "Eight Days Ride to Visit the Noted Apache Chief Cochise: Interview With the Rocky Mountain King. Apache Camp in the Heart of the Mountains."

The editor concluded the article by assuring his readers that "the terrible Cochise is anxious to bury the hatchet and remain at peace."

The newspaper also reported that the true name of Cochise was Chise, or Cheis, the Apache word for wood. A small farm village later was established on Cuchillo Negro Creek at or near the site of Cochise's camp and named Chise by Bentura Trujillo, an early Hispanic settler who became acquainted with the Apache chief while living near the Apache camp in 1871.

In 1872, another interview with Cochise appeared in several New Mexico and Arizona newspapers. By that spring, Cochise had moved his camp into the southern reaches of the lofty and forested San Mateo Mountains, about twelve miles north of the Canada Alamosa agency.

Here he was visited in March by a delegation of government and military officials headed by Colonel Gordon Granger, commander of the New Mexico Military District, and Nathaniel Pope, New Mexico superintendent of Indian affairs. The newspapers chronicled the visit.

The delegation had the twofold mission of inviting Cochise to meet with President Ulysses S. Grant in Washington, D.C., and to persuade him to settle on a new Apache reservation that was being established along the Tularosa River about seventy miles northwest of Canada Alamosa in present-day Catron County.

Cochise declined the offer to travel to Washington, but told the delegation that they had his permission to take his picture there. (No picture of Cochise is known to exist). He also refused to move to the new reservation.

"I want to live in these mountains," he said. "I do not want to go to Tularosa. The flies in those mountains eat the eyes of the horses. The bad spirits live there. I have drunk of these waters and they have cooled me. I do not want to leave here."

A transcript of the dialogue between Cochise and his visitors, attributed to Henry S. Turrill, an Army assistant surgeon at nearby Fort Craig who attended the meeting, was published in part by several newspapers in New Mexico and Arizona. Cochise's remarks apparently were in his native tongue and translated by an interpreter. This is a portion of the published dialogue:

COCHISE: *What will they do to me when I go to Washington?*
POPE: *They want to talk to you and see what you want and where you want to live. I pledge you my word that you will not be harmed.*
COCHISE: *When God created the Apaches, they were made so that they could sit today by this water, and soon by another, where there was mescal and such things as they want, and they are not used to staying in one place.* POPE: *I want you to go tell the great father in Washington.*

COCHISE: *Here where we live now, children can get fruit and such things that grow here. Maybe in Washington they cannot get it.*

POPE: *In the States you can get all and much more.*

COCHISE: *My father, my uncle and my brothers have died here. If I go to the States can I find them there?*

POPE: *No, but if you keep peace, after you die you will find them.*

COCHISE: *I would much rather live here in the mountains where the grass dies, for when I lay down, if it gets in my hair, I can get it out, and I know that all things are right here.*

GRANGER: *The great father in Washington wants you and Loco and Victorio to go to Washington.*

COCHISE: *I am not a child, and would rather talk to you in this country who know more about here.*

GRANGER: *These are the words of the great father. I cannot say more.*

COCHISE: *Why do you get up so often? What is that for?*

GRANGER: *We are hungry and thirsty, we have nothing to eat or drink.*

COCHISE: *You have been looking for me a long time. Why don't you stay and talk?*

GRANGER: *I am hungry, and have invited Loco and Victorio to come into town and have a feast.*

COCHISE: *I do not want to go. I do not want anything but water. If I feel a little hungry, I can get some corn, but I don't want to go into town.*

GRANGER: *I pledge you my life you are safe. Of what are you afraid?*

COCHISE: *I do not eat meat.*

GRANGER: *There is coffee and sugar for you.*

COCHISE: I would rather talk on top of a mountain than in town.

GRANGER: We both promise you that you will be safe in town.

COCHISE: Women and children may sleep in the corral, but I have been used to going where I pleased. The country was once full of Apaches and they have been crowded out by the white man, so that there are few of us, so that there is no room for us here.

GRANGER: I want to put you in a place where the white man cannot put his foot.

COCHISE: Why can we not have all the mountains among which we talk? They belong to us. My country is full of gold, and they are building towns and driving my people off, and I have to kill a coyote for food. The people who come to this country find gold and get rich, and then complain if I get a horse.

GRANGER (aside): Such is fate.

The conference ended on March 20, 1872, and a few days later Cochise left the agency and led his band back to his stronghold in the Dragoon Mountains in southeast Arizona, where the ailing chief died on June 8, 1874.

Top Left Portrait: Jose Francisco Chaves by Mathew Brady (Courtesy Library of Congress digital ID cwpbh.00624)

Top Right Portrait: Jose M. Gallegos November 1872 photo by Frederick Gutekunst (Courtesy Museum of New Mexico Neg. No. 9882)

Bottom Center Photo: Group of people Plaza at Mesilla, New Mexico 1890 (Courtesy Museum of New Mexico Neg. No. 014578)

THE 1871 MESILLA RIOT
Republicans Vs. Democrats

Trouble was feared when Dona Ana County Democrats and Republicans announced separate plans to hold political rallies on the town plaza of Mesilla, then the county seat, on Sunday afternoon, August 27, 1871. Mesilla businessmen, concerned that the proximity of boisterous rallies could pose a threat to the lives and properties of the predominately Hispanic town of 2000 inhabitants in southern New Mexico, called county political leaders together to work out a compromise.

Since the Democrats had announced their plans first, it was agreed that they would hold their rally on the plaza, while Republicans would rally at the home of John Lemon, one of their leaders, on a street a short distance off the plaza

Both rallies began on schedule that Sunday afternoon, with Democrats whooping it up for Jose Manuel Gallegos, their candidate for delegate to Congress, and Republicans cheering for J. Francisco Chaves, their candidate for the same position. Gallegos, a defrocked Catholic priest, lived in Santa Fe, and Chaves, prominent lawyer and veteran soldier, lived in Albuquerque. Both had served terms in Congress.

The two rallies, during which it was said that alcohol flowed freely, broke up at about 5 o'clock that afternoon, and each political party decided to wind up the festivities by parading around the plaza, or town square. The Democrat procession included a band playing "Marching Through Georgia" to which Civil War tune the Democrats sang a Spanish language political song. Unfortunately, the opposing partisans paraded around the plaza in opposite directions.

When the two processions met head-on in front of the Reynolds and Griggs store, each refused to make way for the other, and heated arguments began between those in the vanguards of the two processions. It was during the height of an argument between Republican John Lemon and Democrat I.N. Kelly that one of the participants, Apolonio Barela, fired his pistol into the air. It proved to be an unintentional signal for the chaos that followed.

Kelly, who was carrying a heavy pick handle, slammed it down on Lemon's head, knocking him down and causing his death. Felicito Arroyas y Lueras, a Republican, then shot Kelly to death, and he in turn was shot and killed by a Democrat. General gunfire quickly erupted, and the nearly 1,000 persons on the plaza stampeded in all directions, trampling slow moving ones under foot as they rushed down narrow streets leading from the plaza.

The Santa Fe *Weekly Post*, on September 2, published a dispatch from its Mesilla correspondent describing the scene: "Men, women and children rushed hither and thither in a state of utter distraction. The dead and wounded fell upon all sides, and non-combatants hurried in every direction for shelter." Members of the two political parties took up positions on the roofs of the homes of Mariano Barela and F. Berkner, which faced each other across the plaza, and continued the shooting. Shots also were exchanged from other rooftops, doorways and windows. The newspaper continued:

> *In some instances persons would arrive from the country perfectly unaware of any difficulty, and upon their appearance were fired upon without warning. Some of them would fall, perhaps mortally wounded, while the more fortunate would make beautiful time, without any regard as to direction, but merely to make the most distance in the shortest time possible.*

Meanwhile, a horseback rider was dispatched to Fort Selden, about 17 miles north of Mesilla, to ask for assistance in quelling the riot. Sent to Mesilla were about 65 troopers of the U.S. 8th Cavalry, who arrived in town after dark and camped on the now quiet plaza.

It was estimated that at least nine persons were killed and between 40 and 50 wounded during the gun battle between Republicans and Democrats. Most of the wounded were treated in private homes.

Judge Hezekiah S. Johnson of Albuquerque was sent south to Mesilla to investigate the riot, but after listening to heated and conflicting accounts for three days, he returned home without taking any action. No charges were ever filed in connection with the deadly gun battle.

Mesilla experienced an exodus of several dozen of its citizens who considered the town unsafe. Some established a colony south of the Mexican border at Ascension, Chihuahua, and others fled west to establish settlements on New Mexico's Mimbres River.

Judge Hezekiah S. Johnson (Courtesy Museum of New Mexico Neg. No. 7590)

Rio Grande River (Courtesy Museum of New Mexico Neg. No. 147563)

SOME RIVER WADERS
Two Wet Feet Tales

Two temporary but flourishing mining camps, known as Rio Mimbres and Brooklyn, stood on opposite banks of the shallow Mimbres River east of Silver City in the early 1870s. The only river crossing in the vicinity was a log that served as a narrow foot bridge.

The Rio Mimbres miners, learning one evening in the fall of 1873 that a dance was in progress across the river in Brooklyn, decided to join the fun. Picking up some gallon jugs of alcoholic spirits, they made their way across the log bridge and headed a short distance down the stream to the other mining camp.

By the time the dance broke up at about three o'clock in the morning, the Rio Mimbres visitors were quite unsteady on their feet and wondering if they could make it home. Their biggest concern was crossing the log bridge that spanned the river.

The drunk miners asked a white-haired justice of the peace to lead them home across the bridge. The judge, a dignified looking man who had partaken of his share of the spirits, and maybe more than his share, agreed to lead the way.

The unsteady judge, followed by about twenty of the stumbling Rio Mimbrites, headed upstream towards the bridge. A bright moon that night cast the shadow of a tall cottonwood tree across the river, and the judge thought the shadow was the log bridge.

Carefully balancing himself with outstretched arms, and slowly placing one foot in front of the other, he walked through the water on the shadow of the tree. The miners, in single file, followed him carefully, each exercising the same care.

When the last man had crossed the shadow to the opposite bank, the miners congratulated themselves on having crossed the bridge without anybody falling off. There was some confusion, however, on why their boots were filled with water.

True or not, the story was published in the November 15, 1873 issue of *Mining Life*, a Silver City weekly newspaper.

John B. Bail, a resident of Mesilla, was asked by his wife in the spring of 1875 to go hunt some rabbits for a stew she planned to make. Shouldering his gun, he walked west out of town and hunted in vain up and down the east bank of the Rio Grande.

Thinking the hunting might be better on the other side of the river, he stripped off all his clothing, tied it into a bundle, and waded and swam to the West bank of the river with the bundle held over his head to keep it dry.

Upon reaching the west bank of the river, he put his clothing back on, but found to his dismay that his shoes and socks were missing. They had fallen out of the bundle and had been swept away by the river.

Bail, a man of tender feet, knew that he couldn't walk barefooted across the rocky and thorny terrain that lay between him and his Mesilla home. He sat down on the riverbank, near the stagecoach route that led more than 100 miles northwest to Silver City, and pondered his predicament.

After a while, a westbound stagecoach out of Mesilla came rumbling down the road and drew to a halt.

"Where in hell are you going in your bare feet?" the driver, Font Williams, shouted to the man on the riverbank. Bail replied that he wasn't going anywhere, that he had lost his shoes and couldn't walk home.

Williams suggested that he climb aboard the coach and ride to Silver City, the next stop, and wait there for the next eastbound coach to Mesilla.

Bail thought this was a good idea, and climbed aboard. Upon reaching Silver City, Bail walked around town for a day or two in his bare feet, which attracted the attention of a reporter for the Grant County *Herald*, which published an account of his ordeal on May 2, 1875.

Bail apparently had a lot of explaining to do when he arrived home sans rabbits, sans shoes, and a story about having been all the way to Silver City and back.

Plaza Mesilla, New Mexico. (Courtesy Museum of New Mexico Neg. No. 37917)

Silver City, New Mexico 1879 Photo by Alfred S. Addis
(Courtesy Museum of New Mexico Neg. No. 100556)

THE GRANT COUNTY REBELLION
A Revolt Against Santa Fe Rule

New Mexico almost became a much smaller state. In 1876, Silver City, seat of Grant County, had been in existence only six years when its citizens voted overwhelmingly to detach the county from New Mexico and attach it instead to neighboring Arizona. Such a drastic move required more than mere countywide balloting, however.

Established in 1868, Grant County covered the entire southwest corner of New Mexico, extending south from Socorro County to the Mexican border, and west from Dona Ana County to the Arizona border. The county contained the richest mining districts in New Mexico, and Silver City was emerging as a mining boomtown.

Silver City residents resented the fact that political leaders in Santa Fe had failed to approve their requests for an act of incorporation for the city and the establishment of a public schools system. They also resented the fact that representation in the territorial legislature had been reapportioned so that Grant, Dona Ana and Lincoln counties, with a combined population of more than 8,000, had been lumped together with only two representatives.

The Grant County *Herald* at Silver City published a front page editorial on September 16, 1876, headlined "A Contemplated Political Change" and calling for the annexation of Grant County by Arizona along with a public meeting to discuss the proposal. The editorial said in part:

*If New Mexico should lose her richest county she can charge
it to the dictatorial and corrupt spirit of a few men in Santa Fe,
who have come to the conclusion that they alone are the Com-
monwealth, and have the right to dictate the policy of the Territory and direct her legislation in their own selfish interests.*

The weekly newspaper published another article on September 28
saying that its editorial had caused "a ripple of excitement in southern New Mexico," and that even residents of Dona Ana County were
talking "secession."

The Herald said that annexation of Grant County by Arizona
"would free us from a selfish clique who give us only bad laws, unequal
representation, heavy taxes and no voice in public affairs." The newspaper added that Arizona had better laws than New Mexico, lower
taxes and was attracting more emigrants. Arizona also had an excellent
school system, the newspaper said, adding that New Mexico "was without any school system worthy of the name."

On September 30, the newspaper published a notice, signed by
sixty-four leading citizens, calling a public meeting for October 4 to
discuss the move to Arizona.

A large crowd attended the October 4 meeting, during which officers
were elected and a resolutions committee organized. The committee issued a statement saying that "New Mexico was badly governed and the
laws enacted by our territory are unsuited to our wants." Arizona laws
were better suited for the needs of a mining town, the statement said,
and Silver City was geographically nearer the center of population and
capital (Tucson) of Arizona than of New Mexico.

A countywide election was set for November 4 for citizens to vote
on whether the county should stay in New Mexico or join Arizona. On
election day, each voter was handed a ballot reading "Annexation to
Arizona – Yes or No."

The Silver City newspaper reported after the election that annexation had carried unanimously in almost every precinct, with only about twenty "no" votes cast in the entire county. This did not settle the matter, however. The U.S. Congress had to approve the annexation.

A resolution was introduced in Congress a year later requesting that Grant County, New Mexico, be annexed to Arizona Territory. It was referred to the Committee on Territories, where it promptly died.

The efforts of the Grant County citizens were not in vain, however. Their threat of secession caused Santa Fe politicians to sit up and take notice, and Silver City was soon granted privileges not enjoyed by any other municipality in New Mexico. The 1878 New Mexico legislature passed an act that approved incorporation of Silver City and that included provisions for the election of city officials and the collecting of taxes, and in 1882 the legislature permitted Silver City to establish the first independent school district in New Mexico.

Silver City, A large crowd gathers for a event 1889 Photo by The Reverend Ruben E. Pierce (Courtesy Silver City Museum Neg. No. 1269)

Group in front of railroad locomotive, New Mexico 1890 Photo by J. N. Furlong
(Courtesy Museum of New Mexico Neg. No. 146453)

WORKING ON THE RAILROAD
A Freak Accident And A Suspicious Charter

Last Saturday an iron horse on the Santa Fe road near Florida station got loose from its keeper, and in its wild fury went prancing over the plains doing considerable damage before it could be captured.

Thus began an article in an 1884 issue of the *Southwest Sentinel,* a weekly Silver City newspaper, telling of a freak accident on the railroad line between the southern New Mexico communities of Hatch and Deming. The accident occurred on June 14, 1884, on a forty-six mile stretch of the Atchison, Topeka and Santa Fe Railroad system.

A westbound freight train, bound from Hatch southwest to Deming, had reached a point about twenty miles from Hatch when the engineer suddenly realized that he had "missed his calculations," as the newspaper said, and realized that he was on a collision course with a passenger train heading northeast from Deming. He decided that quick steps were needed to warn the oncoming train.

The engineer stopped the freight train, and he and the fireman got out and quickly unbuckled the locomotive from the freight cars. Climbing back into the cab of the unencumbered locomotive, they sped southwest to the Florida station north of Deming.

Upon reaching Florida, about fifteen miles north of Deming, the engineer and fireman told the stationmaster to send a flagman down the tracks to flag down the approaching passenger train. The flagman was dispatched on his mission, and the engineer and fireman climbed back into their locomotive and started backing it towards the standing freight cars they had left behind.

But once again the engineer missed his calculations. He soon real-ized that the locomotive was backing so fast that he would not be able to bring it to a halt before reaching the standing freight cars. He and the fireman bailed out of the locomotive just before it crashed into them.

The impact of the collision jolted the locomotive's mechanism into a forward position, and the engineer and fireman watched helplessly as their "iron horse" gathered speed and took off towards Florida with nobody aboard.

The unmanned locomotive sped past the startled stationmaster at Florida, passed the flagman who was running down the tracks to flag down the passenger train, and crashed head-on with the approaching passenger train's locomotive.

"Fortunately, no one was hurt," the Silver City newspaper said. "Two coaches of the passenger train, directly behind the locomotive, were filled with soldiers, but neither of them sustained any material damage, but the express car just behind them was completely wrecked. It is needless to say that both locomotives are laid up for repairs."

"Deming Damned -- Not With Faint Praise, But By The Hearty Condemnation Of All Good Citizens" exclaimed a headline in the Silver City *Enterprise* on July 13, 1883, describing a very suspicious chartered train ride by several dozen residents of a neighboring town.

The Silver City newspaper contended that sixty Deming residents had sneaked into Silver City the night before on a special train they had chartered for the express purpose of lynching William H. "Doc" Kane, a Deming saloonkeeper who was hiding out in the city. The Deming citizens denied the accusation, contending that they had chartered the train merely to take them on a "moonlight excursion" to Silver City.

Silver City, The William H. Kane House on Kelly Street, 1890 Contributed by Clara Ward(Courtesy Silver City Museum Neg. No. 58)

But why, then, asked Silver City newspaper, did the chartered train creep quietly into town at 10:30 that evening with the headlight turned off and the bell and whistle silent? Why did it stop before it reached the depot and discharge armed passengers? Just a moonlight excursion, repeated the Deming citizens, threatening to sue Silver City because some of the passengers had been arrested.

Kane had first aroused the ire of Deming residents the previous May when he shot and killed Richard "Three Finger Dick" Tabler, a Southern Pacific Railroad conductor, during a drunken row in Mrs. Catherine Downey's lodging house in Deming. Released on a $5,000 bond, and fearing for his safety, he went north to Silver City.

Returning to Deming in July, he got drunk, entered a saloon owned by John S. Crouch, and began abusing him and calling him names. Both men fired at each other but missed, and Crouch hit Kane on the head with his revolver, knocking him to the floor. Kane slept for a while on the floor, then got up and headed back to Silver City.

Deming citizens decided that they had had enough of Doc Kane by this time, and a group of them decided to go to Silver City and hang him. They passed a hat, collected about $100, and used the money to charter a train and travel the forty-seven miles north to Silver City on the recently completed Silver City, Deming and Pacific narrow gauge line About sixty armed men boarded the train on July 12, 1883, and when the train reached the outskirts of Silver City that night, about twenty of them got off and began filtering through the streets looking for Kane.

M.H. Horn, the Silver City town marshal, was tipped off about the oncoming visitors, however, and he placed Kane in protective custody, gathered some deputies around him, and proceeded to arrest eight of the visitors on the streets. One of them escaped, ran back to the train and gave the alarm, and the engineer sounded the whistle as a warning for those passengers still on the streets. All but the seven who were arrested ran back to the train and climbed aboard. The train departed in a hurry at 2 in the morning.

Deming then threatened to file suit against Silver City for false imprisonment of seven of its citizens, claiming that sixty of them had taken a moonlight excursion to Silver City to enjoy the sights, but that the Silver City marshal had prevented them from "enjoying the simple privilege of free, honest and peaceable citizens while in Silver City."

The seven Deming men who were arrested and jailed were charged with unlawful assembly, carrying concealed weapons and attempting to incite a riot. They were released when the grand jury failed to indict them.

Silver City, Engine No. 71 (Courtesy Silver City Museum Neg. No. 411)

Silver City, Grant County Jail, 1900 (Courtesy Silver City Museum Neg. No. 178)

Top Left: Portrait Former Sea Captain John G. Clancey (Courtesy R.G. McCubbin Collection)
Top Right Portrait: Former Priest Alexander Grzelachowski (Courtesy Museum of New Mexico Neg. No. 122898)
Bottom Photo: Sheep ranch, New Mexico (Courtesy Museum of New Mexico Neg. No. 053805)

TWO PUERTO DE LUNA PIONEERS:

A Former Sea Captain And A Former Priest

It was late in the afternoon on Christmas Day in 1880 that a spring wagon carrying four shackled prisoners, including Billy the Kid, broke down and became stranded at the Celso Baca crossing of the Pecos River, where the town of Santa Rosa is located today. Escorting the prisoners north to Las Vegas at the time were Pat Garrett, sheriff-elect of Lincoln County, and four armed guards.

The Kid and his companions, Dave Rudabaugh, Billy Wilson and Tom Pickett, members of an outlaw gang, had been captured by Garrett and a posse two days before at a small rock house at Stinking Springs, east of Fort Sumner, at which time one of the outlaws, Charlie Bowdre, had been killed. The captured men had been taken first to Fort Sumner, where they were placed in a borrowed wagon for the trip north up the Pecos River Valley to Las Vegas, the nearest rail station, a distance of about one hundred miles.

The lawmen and their prisoners paused at the Pecos River community of Puerto de Luna, where they were furnished a Christmas dinner at the spacious home and store of Alexander Grzelachowski, prominent merchant and former Catholic priest. They left Puerto de Luna at about 4 o'clock that afternoon and had traveled ten miles north when the wagon broke down at the river crossing when a faulty rear wheel fell off.

The accident proved a dilemma for the stranded party, as they were about sixty miles short of their destination in a sparsely settled region on a primitive road that handled but little traffic. Repairing the disabled wagon seemed out of the question.

Fortunately, a lone wagon approached them from the north, driven by a man who offered his assistance by exchanging wagons with them. The shackled prisoners were placed in the good wagon, which continued north, while the Good Samaritan drove the crippled wagon (with a pole holding up the wheel-less rear corner) south to Puerto de Luna.

Garrett, in writing of the episode, referred to his benefactor as "Captain Clarency," but his true name was Captain John G. Clancey, a former New England sea captain who had established a large sheep ranch south of Puerto de Luna.

The remarkable story of how a New England sea captain became a New Mexico sheep rancher was eventually related by his sons, John J. and Carlos C. Clancey, in a series of interviews. Both sons had distinguished careers in public service.

Their father, Captain John George Clancey, was born in Brattleboro, Vermont, on November 30, 1836. He left home when he was 16 or 17 years old and shipped out as a cabin boy on a sailing vessel, making two trips around Cape Horn before earning enough to enroll in a bookkeeping course at a Boston school. Following his graduation, he worked as a bookkeeper at Havana, Cuba, where he learned to speak Spanish.

Capt. John G. Clancey on his horse "Apache" with dog named "Mose"
Puerto de Luna, New Mexico 1883 (Courtesy R.G. McCubbin Collection)

Clancey returned to sea after a short stay in Havana, serving 18 years as an official of various shipping lines and as captain of the sailing ship *Polynesia*. Leaving the shipping business, he settled in San Francisco and bought a seat on the stock exchange.

While in California he paid $100 for a deed to Guadalupe Island, in the Pacific about 260 miles southwest of San Diego, and began raising Angora goats there until he learned that the small island belonged to Mexico rather than the United States. He sold the island for $10,000 and returned to San Francisco.

Learning that New Mexico had large expanses of open range suitable for the raising of sheep, Clancey decided to go look for himself. Traveling alone, riding one horse and leading a pack horse behind, he headed east to New Mexico in 1873 with $50,000 in cash concealed in his belt.

While crossing Arizona he purchased from a U.S. cavalry officer a horse that had been trained to chase down Indians. His sons said that the cavalry horse, named Apache, caused trouble thereafter by taking out after any person who happened to be wearing bright-colored clothing. Clancey visited Las Vegas during his quest for a suitable New Mexico sheep ranch, and here he met Alexander Grzelachowski, who was in the process of selling his mercantile business there and moving south to Puerto de Luna. He suggested that Clancey examine the Pecos Valley region around Puerto de Luna as a possible site for a sheep ranch.

First settled in the early 1860s by Hispanic farmers and ranchers, Puerto de Luna was designated the seat of newly-created Guadalupe County in 1891. Although the Spanish name of the village was once translated as Gateway to the Moon, a more likely and accepted translation is Luna's Gap, in reference to an early Hispanic settler of the Luna family. About ten years later, the seat was moved ten miles north to the now-bustling railroad community of Santa Rosa.

After visiting the region, Clancey decided that an area along Alamogordo Creek, where that stream flows into the Pecos River south of Puerto de Luna, looked promising. He bought 500 sheep from Grzelachowski and went into business.

Clancey drove his first flock of sheep north to Pueblo, Colorado, where he sold them for $17,000. He also sold his mules and wagons there, and returned to San Francisco and his seat on the stock exchange. His stay there was a short one, however, for in 1878 he sold his seat on the stock exchange and headed back to New Mexico, stopping in Arizona to buy 12,000 sheep that he trailed to his holdings on Alamogordo Creek.

Clancey married Mary Gurule of Puerto de Luria, and the two lived in a small dugout on his ranch pending completion of a large home. He built the first dam on Alamogordo Creek and grew alfalfa in irrigated fields along the stream.

The ranch house, completed in about 1888, was a rambling adobe structure with two towers that gave it the appearance of a fort. The home included an inner patio, portals, walled gardens and a walled corral.

Clancey sold his ranch holdings in 1915, at the age of 79, and died a year later.

Photo of the Clancey home near Puerto de Luna, New Mexico 1883 (Courtesy of R.G. McCubbin Collection)

The career of Alexander Grzelachowski, like that of John G. Clancey, was one of unusual contrasts. Born in 1824 in Gracina, Poland, Grzelachowski chose to become a Roman Catholic priest while his father and two brothers opted for distinguished military careers. After completing his studies in a European seminary, probably in France, he was recruited for service in the United States.

Grzelachowski first saw service in the United States in 1850 as resident pastor of a church in Avon, Lorain County, Ohio. While there he met the Rev. Jean B. Lamy, soon to become the first Bishop of Santa Fe, and he accompanied Lamy to Santa Fe in 1851.

During the 1850s he served as pastor of the New Mexico communities of San Miguel, Las Vegas and Manzano and the Indian pueblos of Cochiti, Santo Domingo and San Felipe. He was granted U.S. citizenship in 1855.

Grzelachowski left the priesthood in 1858 to enter the more profitable business world. He established a store at Sapello, north of Las Vegas, and then a large mercantile firm on the Las Vegas plaza. He also operated military wagon supply trains.

During the Civil War he served as military chaplain to New Mexico Volunteers and was credited with helping to guide a force of Colorado Volunteers through the mountains to attack and destroy the Confederate wagon train during the 1862 Battle of Glorieta.

While living in Las Vegas he met an attractive young woman, Secundina C. de Baca, who became his recognized common-law wife and mother of his nine children. (The belief has been expressed that some or all of the children were adopted.)

Grzelachowski moved to Puerto de Luna in 1874 and erected a large, L-shaped structure in the center of the village that served as his home, mercantile store and warehouse. He spent the remainder of his life there as a merchant and sheep rancher.

During his life as a leading citizen of Puerto de Luna, Grzelachowski was known to his Hispanic neighbors as Don Alejandro and Padre Polaco. He died in 1896 of injuries suffered when the horse-drawn wagon he was driving overturned.

The elaborate Clancey home, which straddled the Guadalupe-De-Baca County line, gradually faded away into ruins, but much of the Grzelachowski home, in the center of Puerto de Luna, remains intact today as a New Mexico registered cultural property.

John G. Clancey, Puero de Luna, New Mexico 1901 Photo by J.N. Furlong
(Courtesy Museum of New Mexico Neg. No. 91358)

Group of men includes Capt. John C. Clancey seated first chair far right. (Courtesy of R.G. McCubbin Collection)

Alexander Grzelachowski home, Puerto de Luna, New Mexico 1955 Photo by Howard Bryan

Quarai Mission Church, Salinas National Monument, New Mexico 1954 (Courtesy Museum of New Mexico Neg. No. 006653)

SOME WEIRD NEW MEXICO TALES
Ghosts, Midgets, Giants And Ufos

Ghost Sighting At Quarai Mission

An Illinois family, traveling around New Mexico in 1913 in a luxuriously equipped prairie schooner, told of seeing a strange apparition while camped outside the centuries old Quarai mission church ruins near the southeast slopes of the Manzano Mountains about sixty miles southeast of Albuquerque. Their story was published in the Albuquerque *Evening Herald* on November 28, 1913.

Wilbur S. Saener, who said his home was near Minonk, Illinois, wrote to the newspaper from Willard, New Mexico, that he had brought his wife to New Mexico for her health and that they were accompanied by their young daughter. Told of the spectacular ruins of the old mission church, they decided to go see them for themselves. Built in about 1629 to serve an Indian pueblo, the church and pueblo were abandoned in about 1674.

This is how Saener described what they saw at the ruins:

> *We camped two nights at the old mission and many were the thoughts of a religious turn that passed through our minds as we lay there at night and gazed into the shadows of the ruins of this house of worship. Nothing occurred during the first night out of the ordinary, but what I saw on the second night will always remain fresh in my memory. My family and myself will never be able to blot it from memory.*

I was restless for some reason and got up, and through one of the openings in the end of the ruined edifice I saw a brilliant, blue-white light, and in the center of the light stood the figure of a man, apparently a Spaniard, but dressed in the uniform of a French soldier. Thinking my eyes deceived me, I called my family and they, too, saw the ghostly light and soldier.

Three times he pointed a finger and said, "Siste, viator," which is Latin for 'stop, visitor,' And of a sudden the light and the man disappeared.

The Illinois family also disappeared from the scene. The Quarai mission church ruins, with towering red sandstone walls among the low ruins of the Indian pueblo it served, are preserved today as part of the Salinas National Monument.

The Mysterious Ghost Woman

Cowboys in the southwestern part of New Mexico were telling strange stories in 1906 about a beautiful young "ghost woman" on a fleet bay horse who would appear before them on the open ranges by day and by night and then vanish as mysteriously as she had come. The cowboys described her as a beautiful young lady, tall and slender, her skin tanned by the sun. They said she wore a khaki-colored riding suit, patent leather riding boots and silver spurs.

Women were few and far between on New Mexico's open ranges in those days, and reported sightings of a mysterious woman riding the range on horseback attracted the attention of various newspapers. Many believed that she was a supernatural being.

Pete Bianca, a cowboy in the Deming area, gave the first report of the "ghost woman" in May, 1906. He said he was approaching the Mimbres River crossing of the old Butterfield Trail north of Deming when he noticed a beautiful young woman cantering her horse on the trail ahead of him. She dismounted at the crossing, he said, drank from the stream, and rode on down the trail towards Dan Taylor's ranch.

Bianca said he followed her to the Taylor ranch where he found Taylor, a bachelor, mending a saddle. He said he asked Taylor about the young woman who had just ridden to his ranch, and Taylor answered that he had not seen any young woman, and that there were none within miles of his ranch.

After some discussion, Bianca took Taylor down the trail a short distance and showed him the hoof prints of the woman's horse. But the tracks disappeared when they reached a point about one hundred yards from the ranch house. No further trace of the woman could be found.

The next reported sighting of the "ghost woman" came about a week later when Ed Tuttle, a csttleman, said that he was approaching the copper mining town of Santa Rita when he caught up with and passed a beautiful young lady on a bay horse. He said he raised his hat to her as he passed, but that she did not seem to notice his presence. He said he asked about her in Santa Rita, but nobody had seen her or knew anything about her.

Later, a corporal at nearby Fort Bayard told Tuttle that he had ridden past the woman on a road near the mining town of Georgetown. He said he spoke to her and raised his hat, believing her to be an officer's wife, and that she wheeled her horse around without a word and galloped off in the opposite direction.

"And she disappeared right in the middle of the road as I was watching her," the corporal said.

Bert Cooper said he was riding the range south of the 0 Bar 0 Ranch one moonlit night when he saw a young woman on horseback on a small rise on the trail about two hundred yards ahead of him. He said she rode off as he sped towards her, but that she left him far behind even though he was riding one of the fastest cow ponies in the region.

Navajo Andrews, another cowboy, reported that he had ridden to within one hundred yards of the woman near the foot of the Florida Mountains south of Deming. She waved to him, he said, and then disappeared in the direction of the Crazy S Ranch.

Fletch Burke reported that he was rounding up some calves on the range one night when the women rode up almost next to him. He spoke to her, he said, but she rode off without answering.

The last report of the "ghost woman," as reported in newspapers at the time, came early in September, 1906, when three Flying Y Ranch cowboys, Sam Teener, Manuelo Yeros and Mont Steen, reported seeing her at the edge of the towering rock pillar formations north of Deming known as the City of Rocks

When they first saw her, Teener said, she was sitting on her bay horse and gazing intently at the island of strange rock formations. She had removed her hat, he said, and her long brown hair was blowing about her face. She was holding a hairpin in her teeth, and was preparing to fasten a loose strand of her hair.

The three cowboys began closing in on her from three sides, and Teener said he got close enough to her to say "Good morning." Without answering, he said, she put spurs to her horse and disappeared quickly behind a large boulder that stood alone some distance from the City of Rocks. The cowboys followed her, but could find no trace of the woman or her horse tracks behind the boulder.

Teener said he went back to the spot where they had first seen the "ghost woman." Noticing a tiny object on the ground, he leaned over and picked it up.

It was a hairpin.

The Midgets and the Giant

Some Socorro County ranchers in the 1880s claimed that a race of midgets, human beings less than three feet tall, inhabited remote areas of the San Mateo Mountains. Upon occasion, they said, they would get glimpses of these little people scampering up and down the mountainside and leaping from rock to rock. At about the same time, some ranchers farther south claimed that a giant of a man was seen occasionally roaming through the San Andres Mountains.

Dr. W.T. Strachan of Albuquerque reported in 1866 that while prospecting on the southwest slopes of the nearby Sandia Mountains he climed into a small opening in some rocks and found himself in a large cave. In the cave, he said, he found the skeleton of a giant of a man.

Strachan said he picked up one of the large bones and carried it to Albuquerque where medical examiners pronounced it to be "the first phalanx of the little finger of a man who must have been at least forty feet tall, nine feet across the shoulders, and weighed about 3600 pounds."

The Albuquerque man took the "giant's little finger" to Santa Fe and displayed it in Frank Green's Eldorado Saloon, where it was viewed by hundreds of curious Santa Fe residents. The *New Mexican* at Santa Fe reported on May 18, 1866, that Strachan was "a gentleman of the strictest veracity" since he was a member of the New Mexico Legislature.

Early UFO Sightings?

Some residents of Galisteo Junction, now the village of Lamy south of Santa Fe, reported in 1880 that they saw a large, balloonlike airship pass over the community and that it appeared to be filled with foreigners who were having a loud party. Their account was published in the Daily *New Mexican* at Santa Fe on March 28, 1880.

According to the article, the telegraph operator at Galisteo Junction and two or three friends were taking a short walk on the night of March 26 when they were startled by the sounds of voices above them. Looking up, they saw a large, balloonlike object sailing in from the west. The article said:

> As it rapidly approached, the voices became more distinct but were entirely unintelligible. Loud shouts, in a language unknown to any of the party, were constantly given, evidently with a desire to attract attention.
>
> The air machine appeared to be entirely under the control of the occupants, and appeared to be guided by a large, fanlike apparatus. The party seemed to be enjoying themselves as laughter and occasional strains of music were heard.

The observers said the balloon was monstrous in size, was in the shape of a fish, and decorated with fanciful and elegant characters, while the car, as near as could be determined, contained eight or ten persons. The article continued:

> Another peculiar feature of the air machine was that the occupants could evidently sail it at any height, as soon as passing over the Junction it assumed a great height and moved off very rapidly toward the east.

The observers claimed that several objects were dropped from the airship, including a flower, a fine slip of paper containing characters similar to those found on Japanese tea chests, and an earthenware cup of peculiar workmanship. These, they said, were quickly purchased by a curio collector, who believed the balloon came from Asia.

The Albuquerque *Daily Citizen*, on September 5, 1891, published a letter from Captain A.M. Swan of Albuquerque telling of some strange airships he claimed to have seen two nights before while visiting at Coyote Springs in the Manzano Mountain foothills east of the city.

Swan wrote that he saw the phenomenon on the evening of September 3 while sitting with L.D. Dodson in front of Ed Propper's house at the springs, and that it began about eight o'clock when a brilliant light appeared over the Manzanos and mounted rapidly into the sky.

His letter to the newspaper makes it rather difficult to visualize what Swan was describing:

As it (the light) mounted rapidly into the horizon we soon discovered what appeared to be a bright star following it, but as it neared our point of observation (we) found that it was connected with the larger body.

The singular thing, however, was the fact that what appeared to be a series of electric arc lights constituted a straight base line that was to our view many feet long. From near, but not quite at each end, was apparently an elongated half circle composed of the same dim lights.

From the apex of this circle there appeared to be a long rod covered with dim lights to the outer end, where appeared a brilliant light. This pole, or whatever it was, seemed to be under intelligent direction, and to be used as a rudder or steering apparatus. The phenomenon was moving in the face of the wind, and would frequently tack in the same way that ships tack when running in the eye of the wind.

Swan wrote that he observed this strange sight for more than an hour, at which time a similar phenomenon appeared from the southwest, and the two began to approach each other at quite a rapid speed, but that clouds obscured his vision when the two began to meet. He theorized that the objects were some kind of aerial ships under the control of men skilled in their management.

The *Citizen* published Swan's letter under headlines reading: "Strange Mid-Air Ships: Wonderful Effect of Coyote Water on Captain Swan."

Strange Animal Tales

The *New Mexican* at Santa Fe reported in 1869 that a giant snake was killing and eating cattle on George Martin's ranch at Cerrillos, south of the city.

"It is described as being twelve feet in length, about five inches between the eyes and of a dark color," the newspaper reported on August 17. "That it is possessed of immense strength was proven by its killing a two-year-old steer a short time since by a single blow with its tail, and it has during the present summer killed and swallowed whole a number of calves belonging to Mr. Martin."

The article said that the powerful serpent attacked its victims in a most unusual manner, explaining:

> It entwines its head in the tall grass in such a manner as to get a hold, and from this position throws its tail and body towards its prey with terrible force.

The resulting concussion sometimes caused the victim to break up into pieces, the article claimed. It concluded:

> *These facts are of such a strange nature that we should feel delicate about giving them publicly were it not that they are vouched for by the best authority.*

Two Albuquerque hunters claimed in 1885 that they had captured a curious animal known as a "prox" during a hunting trip in the Sandia Mountains east of the city. The hunters, Thomas Isherwood and Sam Bagnel, told newspapers that the prox was an animal that had rarely been seen and, with one exception, had never before been taken alive.

The prox, according to the hunters, was unusual "in having the legs on one side much shorter than those on the other side, a peculiarity which enables it to run around hillsides with such great rapidity that it is a thing next to impossible to overtake it."

Isherwood, however, said he conceived the idea of heading off the prox and turning it around "so that the shorter legs would come on the downhill side." The plan worked perfectly, he said, for no sooner was the prox turned around than it rolled over and over and right into a bag Bagnel was holding at the foot of the hill.

The hunters said that the only other prox taken alive was one that had been captured by a member of the U.S. Thirteenth Infantry and which was described in the Smithsonian report of 1875.

The Longest and Deadliest Prize Fight

A Colorado newspaper correspondent, while traveling through New Mexico in the summer of 1868, claimed that he witnessed what might rank as the longest and most brutal prizefight in history. The "strictly private" bout was said to have occurred before a large crowd in an open field near Albuquerque.

Charles Johnson, a correspondent for the *Denver News*, wrote that he was traveling north through New Mexico when he met a large group of men on the road about 35 miles from Albuquerque. Recognizing one of the men, he asked him what was going on, and the man replied, after some hesitation, that they were staging a hush-hush prizefight between a man identified only as "Jack" and a Colorado fighter identified only as "Duffey."

Jack had already arrived on the scene and was sitting in a carriage waiting for Duffey to make an appearance, Johnson wrote, and Duffey soon arrived to begin the match. The bets were running high, and the stakes were estimated at $5,000. Here is how the Denver newsman described the prizefight, which he said occurred on June 28, 1868:

They fought 185 rounds, occupying six hours and 19 minutes.

The left side of Duffey's head was fearfully swollen, his left eye closed, his right eye nearly so, two ribs broken, and his left arm useless.

Jack's head was all cut to pieces. He was totally blind the last two rounds, his nose knocked on the left side of his face, three teeth knocked out, two ribs broken and his left arm useless.

He presented a horrible appearance. He died ten minutes after the fight was over.

Duffey was unable to walk, the newsman wrote, and had to be carried from the field.

"I should not have written this," Johnson wrote, adding that he was prompted to do so only because one of the participants died and the other had a Colorado background.

The *New Mexican*, which republished the Denver *News* article on July 21, 1868, noted that the Denver writer had said that the prizefight occurred "on the road 35 miles from Albuquerque" but failed to say whether it was north or south of Albuquerque. But the newspaper noted that some Santa Fe residents, returning home from Albuquerque, had noticed a trampled and blood-stained field 35 miles north of Albuquerque.

Frozen Soldiers

A prospector visited the United States Forest Service offices in Albuquerque in the 1940s to report that he had found the intact bodies of two uniformed Civil War soldiers frozen in perpetual ice in the rugged malpais country near Grants, New Mexico. Perpetual ice caves exist in the lava beds, and the original Fort Wingate was located during the Civil War period along the west edge of the malpais south of Grants. No effort was made to verify the prospector's claim, however.

Capt. Jack Crawford "The Poet Scout" (Courtesy Museum of New Mexico Neg. No. 163480)

THE POET SCOUT
John "Captain Jack" Crawford

Medium in stature and form, slight limp in walking, brown hair worn long and falling upon his shoulders, prominent mustache of the same color, bluish-gray eyes penetrating and full of expression, genial in his salutation and a grasp indicative of frankness.

That is the way the Santa Fe *Daily* Democrat described 34-year-old John Wallace Crawford, familiarly known as "Captain Jack, the Poet Scout," in an interview with the colorful figure published on January 27, 1882. The frontiersman was living at the time at Fort Craig, a military post on the west bank of the Rio Grande in south central New Mexico.

In both physical appearance and in his fringed buckskin attire, Crawford closely resembled his old friend, William F. "Buffalo Bill" Cody, with whom he served as a scout on the northern plains before settling in New Mexico. But unlike Cody, Wallace preferred a writing career to the career of a Wild West showman.

Crawford was born in Donegal County, Ireland, on March 4, 1847, the son of Scottish refugees. His father, a heavy drinker who caused family problems, emigrated to the United States in 1854, leaving his wife and children behind.

Arriving in the United States in 1858 in search of her husband was Mrs. Susan Wallace Crawford, a direct descendant of Sir William Wallace, the famous 14th Century Scottish hero. She found him living at Minerville, Pennsylvania, and sent for their children in Ireland when he promised to reform.

John W. Crawford was eleven years old when he joined his family in Pennsylvania and began working in some coal mines at a salary of $1.75 a week. During the Civil War, since Crawford was a teenager with no formal education, he ran away from home and enlisted in the 48th Pennsylvania Infantry. He was wounded twice, in 1864 at Spotsylvania and in 1865 at Petersburg, Virginia.

While recovering from his battle wounds in Philadelphia, Crawford was taught to read and write by his nurse, a Sister of Charity, so that he could write letters home. From that time on, writing became a passion with him. After the war, he returned to his Pennsylvania home, and in 1869 he married Mariah Stokes, who became the mother of his four children.

Hoping to pursue a writing career on the western frontier, Crawford headed west to Nebraska in 1875 and served as correspondent for several eastern newspapers. His assignments took him to the Dakota Black Hills, scene of a gold rush, and he was named captain of the Black Hills Rangers, an irregular militia outfit.

Crawford next served as a scout and messenger for General Wesley Merritt and General George Crook during the 1876 Indian campaigns in Montana, and he succeeded Buffalo Bill Cody as chief of scouts for the U.S. Fifth Cavalry when Cody embarked on a show business career. His most famous exploit was carrying urgent dispatches on a 350-mile horseback ride through hostile Indian country in four days.

Upon learning of the death of General George Armstrong Custer at the 1876 Battle of Little Big Horn, Crawford penned the following poem:

Did I hear the news from Custer?
Well, I reckon I did, old pard.
It came like a streak o' lightning,
And you bet, it hit me hard.
I ain't no hand to blubber,
And the briny ain't run for years,
But chalk me down for a lubber,
If I didn't shed regular tears.

Crawford eventually joined up with Cody in his entertainment venture. Buffalo Bill, who was staging western melodramas in various theaters, persuaded Crawford, already becoming known as the poet scout, to join him on his theatrical tours. During intermissions, Crawford read examples of his poetry and lectured against the evils of alcohol, having promised his mother never to drink. Cody called him the only teetotaler scout he had ever met.

The Cody-Crawford partnership ended in 1877 when Crawford was accidentally wounded during the performance of a melodrama at Virginia City, Nevada. Crawford claimed that Cody had stabbed him while drunk, while Buffalo Bill maintained that Crawford had carelessly shot himself.

Crawford settled in New Mexico in 1879 and established a home at Fort Craig, where he lived both before and after the military post's 1885 abandonment by the military. During the early 1880s he served as a scout for U.S. cavalry troops in campaigns against Apache forces led successively by Victorio, Nana and Geronimo.

Residence interior of Captain Jack Crawford, Fort Craig, New Mexico 1883(Courtesy Museum of New Mexico Neg. No. 014512)

Late in 1880, after Victorio and his Apache warriors had crossed the border into Mexico, Crawford was assigned to locate the Apache camp in Mexico and attempt to negotiate surrender terms with the elderly Apache leader. Accompanying Crawford on this diplomatic but dangerous mission were Navajo Charlie, an Apache who knew Victorio well and spoke his language, and Casimero, identified only as "a fearless little Mexican."

Crawford and his two companions came to within a mile of the Apache camp, but Navajo Charlie, without giving any explanation, refused to enter the camp. Crawford, unable to speak the Apache tongue, had to abort the mission. Victorio and most of his followers were killed or captured by Mexican troops two months later.

When interviewed by the Santa Fe newspaper in 1882, Crawford was asked how he managed to follow an Indian trail. He replied:

> *This is very easy. We can tell from the way the grass is bent the direction which has been taken, and experience teaches us how much time has passed since the trail was made.*
>
> *For instance, we examine a blade of grass and see just where it had been broken, and then our knowledge of woodcraft tells us just about how long the sun would take to bring the blade to a certain angle. Thus a scout is able to tell just how many hours start the pursued party has.*

Crawford also explained some of the signals he used, when scouting ahead of a body of soldiers, to communicate with the troops behind him:

> *I ride around in a circle three times, then start off in a straight line. This means for the soldiers to follow at once in my direction.*
>
> *Should I ride but twice around and start to the right, this would mean for the soldiers to march in a contrary direction. In case I made but one circle and rode off, this would indicate that I had seen something and had gone to investigate, and for the soldiers to keep quiet. Of course, there are other signs, but these serve to give an illustration.*

Crawford Family at Officers Quarters, Fort Craig, New Mexico 1890(Courtesy Museum of New Mexico Neg. No. 014511)

In addition to writing poems, plays and short stories, Crawford was engaged in a variety of other pursuits during his two decades in New Mexico. He served as post sutler at Fort Craig prior to its abandonment and as custodian or caretaker after its abandonment. He established a ranch home at San Marcial, a village a short distance north of the fort, and operated ranches at Dripping Springs and Grapevine Springs in the San Andres Mountains to the east. He also had mining interests in the New Mexico mining town of Chloride, southwest of the fort, where his brother, Austin Crawford, had settled.

Some recollections of Crawford and his family life were furnished in 1963 by 78-year-old Charles H. Nattress of Albuquerque, a nephew of the poet scout. Nattress said that his father, William K. Nattress, settled in New Mexico in 1880 and married Lizzie Crawford, one of Captain Jack's sisters. Another sister, Rebecca Crawford, married William James of the Chloride area.

Crawford and his wife were the parents of four children in New Mexico, Nattress said. Their only son, Harry, became a Santa Fe Railway conductor and spent his last years in Albuquerque. A daughter, May Cody Crawford, died of scarlet fever at Fort Craig in 1886 when she was five years old. The other daughters were Eva, who married Dan Reckhart, operator of an assay office in El Paso, where she spent the remainder of her life; and the last surviving daughter was Mrs. May Brechtel, who died in 1962 at Moab, Utah. About Captain Jack, Natress said:

Captain Jack lived in an adobe house at the northeast corner of Fort Craig after the military abandoned the post. We used to ride horseback together, from San Marcial to Chloride, and he told me many stories about his life. He told me the Apaches knew him by his shoulder length hair, and as a scout during the Nana and Geronimo campaigns he disguised himself by rolling his hair up into his hat.

During a visit to Chloride, Crawford told friends and relatives that he could write a poem in fifteen minutes on any subject they suggested. They suggested a poem about miners, and in the allotted time he completed a poem that began:

> *Hear the music of the hammer,*
>
> *As it bounds from rock and drill;*
>
> *See the ore piled near the windlass*
>
> *As it glistens on the hill;*
>
> *Hear the giant cannonading,*
>
> *Throwing out its precious load.*
>
> *And the merry song at evening*
>
> *In the miner's log abode.*

Nattress located an early edition of Crawford's book of poetry, *The Poet Scout*, published in 1886 by Funk and Wagnalls of New York. Written in ink on the flyleaf of the book were these words:

> *To My Wife -- The sun is peeping out again, The clouds are fading fast, While hope is lighting up my sky, and fortune smiles at last. Yours Affectionately, J. W. Crawford, Captain Jack.*

The book originally was published in San Francisco in 1879 with the title *The Poet Scout: Being a Selection of Incidental and Illustrative Verse and Songs.*

Crawford joined the Yukon gold rush in 1898 and returned to the United States two years later to embark on theatrical road trips with his unpublished plays and lectures against drinking, smoking, and dime novel versions of the western frontier. Eventually, he settled in Brooklyn, New York, where he died on February 28, 1917, and was laid to rest in Brooklyn's National Cemetery.

Captain Jack Crawford "The Poet Scout" portrait 1890 (Courtesy Museum of New Mexico Neg. No. 15747)

Victorio, Apache Chieftain (Mimbreno Apache) By H.P. Barnes 1880
(Courtesy Museum of New Mexico Neg. No. 14210)

VICTORIO'S APACHE NEWSPAPER
It Didn't Really Exist

A paches under the leadership of Victorio were on the warpath in southern New Mexico in the spring of 1880 when a Las Cruces editor wrote in his weekly newspaper that he had just received the first issue of a newspaper called *The Apache Chronicle*, said to be "published every moon at the headquarters of General Victorio, commander in chief of the Apache nation, as his official organ."

Simeon H. Newman, the Las Cruces editor, devoted several columns to the alleged Apache publication and its contents in his weekly newspaper, which he called *Thirty Four*, because a Democratic candidate he had backed in Republican dominated Dona Ana County had carried the county by a margin of 34 votes. Newman was well aware of the fact, however, that no such Apache newspaper existed.

Victorio and his followers had been on the warpath since the previous September when they bolted from the Mescalero Apache Reservation near Fort Stanton, New Mexico, soon to be joined by several hundred other Apache raiders. In their raids throughout southern New Mexico they killed numerous settlers, attacked stagecoaches and mail wagons, captured government horses and mules, and defeated or outmaneuvered U.S. cavalry troops that attempted to bring them under control.

Many New Mexico citizens of the region blamed federal Indian policies for the Apache uprising, and were highly critical of Colonel Edward Hatch, New Mexico's district military commander and U.S. cavalry leader, for failing to subdue the Apache raiders and for claiming military accomplishments that apparently did not exist. Their complaints often took the form of ridicule and sarcasm, of which the make-believe Apache newspaper was a prime example.

In articles appearing in *Thirty Four* on April 7, 1880, Newman wrote that his issue of *The Apache Chronicle* was accompanied by a letter of introduction signed by Nane (Nana), "secretary of war for the Apache tribe." Listed as editors of the newspaper, in addition to Nana, were such other Apache leaders as Loco, "secretary of finance;" Raton, "attorney general," and Jose, "chief of medicine and custodian of scalps."

The letter of introduction was dated "San Andres Canyon, Organ Mountains, Third Moon," and read as follows:

> *Editor Thirty Four: By direction of the Commander in Chief, I transmit you advance sheets of The Apache Chronicle, official journal of General Victorio, which find enclosed, with the request that you place same on your exchange list.*
>
> *Owing to the misrepresentations of the Big White Chief Hatch, the impression has been created that he has defeated our great and honorable Chief. In order to eradicate this false impression by giving the truth to the world the publication of the Chronicle has been commenced. (signed) "Nane, secretary of war.*

Subscriptions to the Apache newspaper were said to cost "three scalps per noon."

"A premium is offered for soldier scalps, they being very scarce," the newspaper said. "Citizens scalps taken at a discount, as the market is overstocked."

Some news items from *The Apache Chronicle*:

> *Our brave warriors will be pleased to learn that it is reported that our esteemed friend, Captain (Charles D.) Beyer has been ordered to take the field with a fresh pack team and a large supply of ammunition. This intelligence we hope to be true, for our young warriors have wasted considerable ammunition lately shooting cattle.*

"Nana, Chief of the Warm Spring Apaches" Phot by Ben Wittick
(Courtesy Museum of New Mexico Neg. No. 016321)

We learn from our Palomas friends that the U.S. government intends to remount the 9th Cavalry. This is good news, as our stock is quite poor and we need fresh horses badly.

The warrior who was accidentally wounded during our recent campaign has been taken to the Mescalero Reservation where he is receiving the necessary surgical treatment. Upon his recovery he will rejoin Chief Victorio, having first received the usual presents of rifles, ammunition, blankets, rations, etc.

The buckboard carrying the U.S. mail was taken by our braves last week near Aleman on the Jornada. The driver was, of course, killed. In the mail sack was found an official dispatch from the District Commander to the Secretary of War informing him that "all was quiet on the Jornada."

Another article referred to Hatch as "Old Scratch" and said that Apache braves had tapped a telegraph line and intercepted a message from him to the secretary of war that read:

> *I have the honor to report that the accounts received by you of Indian depredations on the Jornada are base fabrications concocted by interested parties. It is true that a stage driver was brought in dead, but there are grave suspicions that he first robbed the mail and then committed suicide to cover his crime. All is quiet here.*

In publishing an account of *The Apache Chronicle* in his Las Cruces newspaper, the editor noted that the letter of introduction accompanying the sheet and signed by "Nane" bore the unmistakable handwriting of Albert J. Fountain, prominent Mesilla lawyer, journalist and militia leader. It was Fountain, in fact, who conceived, wrote and published the make-believe Apache newspaper as a sarcastic indictment of federal Indian policies in general and Col. Hatch in particular.

Coincidentally, the Las Cruces newspaper detailing *The Apache Chronicle* was issued on the day that Victorio's Apaches were successful in eluding three columns of U.S. cavalry troops, commanded by Hatch, that were attempting to defeat or capture the Apaches in Hembrillo Canyon, high in the San Andres Mountains about 45 miles north of Las Cruces.

Another sarcastic example of civilian discontent with U.S. military operations against the Apaches was a brief article that appeared in *The Black Range*, a weekly newspaper published in the New Mexico mining town of Chloride, on December 7, 1883.

According to this story, an Apache chief visited a U.S. military post and asked the commanding officer for the use of a cannon. The officer, of course, refused the request.

"I suppose you want a cannon to kill my soldiers with," the officer said.

"No," the chief replied, "want cannon to kill cowboys. Kill soldiers with a club."

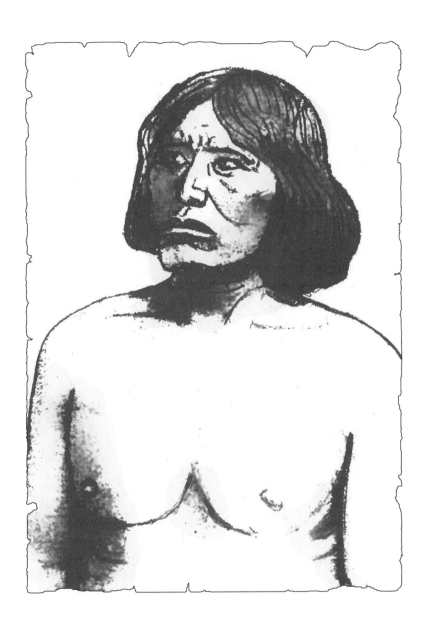

Portrait of Apache Leader Victorio (Courtesy Arizona Historical Society)

Portrait of Albert J. Fountain (Courtesy of Public Domain)

Portrait of Col. Edward Hatch (Courtesy of Public Domain)

Jemez Pueblo, New Mexico 1885 Photo by Ben Wittick
(Courtesy Museum of New Mexico Neg. No. 16097)

AN ANGRY U.S. MAIL CARRIER
Denied Passage Through Indian Pueblo

Neither snow nor rain nor heat nor gloom of night stays these couriers from the swift completion of their appointed rounds.

So says the famous old U.S. Post Office motto, but Indians of Jemez Pueblo stayed a New Mexico mail courier from •the swift completion of his appointed rounds in 1899, and he proceeded to make a federal case of it.

The courier, identified by Albuquerque newspapers only as Hank, drove a mail coach periodically from Albuquerque northwest to Jemez Springs, a distance of about 55 miles. His roundtrips took him through Jemez Pueblo, about 10 miles south of Jemez Springs.

It was on November 12, 1899, when Jemez Pueblo was observing its annual San Diego Feast Day ceremonials, that Hank was met at the southern edge of the pueblo by about 30 armed Indians. They informed him that a secret ceremonial was in progress on the plaza, and that no white man was to enter the pueblo until the ceremonial was over.

The mail driver, becoming impatient, started to whip his horses forward. Immediately, two dozen rifles were aimed at him, and the Indians grabbed his reins and brought the coach to a quick halt.

Hank shouted to the Indians that they would have the federal government to contend with if they did not permit the mail coach to pass through the village at once.

"I am under bond to deliver the mail, and I don't intend to be kept back," he exclaimed.

The Indians went into a huddle, then offered the coach driver a compromise settlement. They offered to unload the mail from the coach, carry it through the pueblo themselves, and deposit it on the north side of the village.

In the meantime, they said, Hank could drive the empty coach around the pueblo on a back road that wound through the mountains, retrieve the mail on the north side of the pueblo, and continue his journey north to Jemez Springs. Hank rejected the compromise offer, saying that he intended to remain with the mail until it reached its destination.

The coach remained motionless at the southern edge of the pueblo for more than three hours while the ceremonials continued on the plaza. Late in the afternoon, when the ceremonials were over, Jose Romero, the pueblo governor, told Hank that he could now drive the mail coach through the pueblo.

After delivering the mail to Jemez Springs, Hank drove quickly back to Albuquerque and told postal authorities that about thirty armed Indians had delayed his progress at Jemez Pueblo.

"He says some of them were covered with bear skins, others with ox hides with horns protruding in a threatening manner, and all had on war paint," the Albuquerque *Daily Citizen* reported on December 6, 1899.

Postal authorities in Washington were notified, and a postal detective was sent to New Mexico to investigate why it was that the U.S. mail could be delayed by an Indian ceremonial. A deputy U.S. marshal was sent to Jemez Pueblo to arrest Jose Romero, the pueblo governor, on a complaint charging him with obstructing the passage of the U.S. mail.

Upon his arrival at the pueblo, the deputy was told by Indians that they would not permit him to arrest the governor and take him to jail. He answered that if they put up any resistance, he would go back to Albuquerque and return with a lot more officers.

The Indians finally agreed to the arrest of their governor, and the deputy took Romero to Albuquerque for an appearance before H.R. Whiting, the U.S. commissioner. The pueblo governor admitted to the facts of the case, and Whiting permitted him to return home after delivering to him a lecture on the powers of the federal government and its insistence that the U.S. mail be delivered without delay or obstruction.

In spite of this episode, three more Jemez Indians were arrested in 1905 on charges of delaying a mail coach while a religious festival was in progress at the pueblo. Charges against them also were dismissed.

Jose Romero and family 1890 Photo by W. H. Jackson (Courtesy Wm. Wroth)

Portrait of Henry R. Whiting (Courtesy of Public Domain)

Man on horseback in the Mogollion Mountains , New Mexico
(Courtesy Museum of New Mexico Neg. No. 4475607)

MODERN NEW MEXICO LEGENDS
Stories Probably Not True

"Bearback" Riding

During the early days, according to some pioneer recollections, a bearded old prospector lived alone in a small cabin he had erected in a remote area of the rugged Mogollon Mountains in southwest New Mexico. He never struck it rich, and couldn't afford to buy a horse, mule or burro. What little gold he found was just enough to buy a few supplies, and to get them he had to hike miles to the nearest village.

One day, as he was prospecting in the mountains, he came across a motherless grizzly bear cub. The little bear appeared to be very friendly, so the prospector decided to take it home and raise it as a pet. Man and bear became devoted friends, and the cub followed him at his heels during his daily prospecting trips in the wilderness.

As time went by, the pet grizzly bear grew larger and larger and eventually reached full size. Nevertheless, it remained devoted to its master.

One day, a brilliant idea struck the prospector.

"If that bear will let me climb on his back and ride him," he thought to himself, "I could ride him on my prospecting trips and even into town to get supplies."

Gingerly, he climbed on the bear's back, put his arms around the bear's neck, and was pleasantly surprised to find that the bear would carry him anyplace he wanted to go. Within a short time, he had the bear trained to respond just like a horse.

Periodically the prospector would ride the bear into the village and tie it to a railing in front of the general store while he went inside to shop for supplies. At first, the villagers were frightened by the sight of the huge bear, but they soon became accustomed to the visits of the prospector and his unusual mount.

One night, as the prospector was sleeping in his cabin, he was awakened by a horrible din. Rushing outside, he found that a wild grizzly bear, even larger than his own, had wandered out of the woods and was engaging his grizzly in battle. The snarling, clawing and biting bears were in a life or death struggle, knocking down small trees in the process.

Without thinking, the prospector rushed into the middle of the affray then quickly realized that to save his own life he was going to have to get out of there in a hurry. He decided that the only way to do this was to jump on his bear and ride to safety.

He jumped on the bear's back, put his arms around its neck, dug his heels into its flanks and shouted "Git." The bear took off with the speed of lightning, the prospector hanging on for dear life.

After the bear had raced down a canyon for a mile or so, the prospector thought he was out of danger, and he started pulling on the bear's neck and shouting "Whoa." But instead of stopping, the bear gathered speed. "Whoa, whoa," the prospector kept shouting, but the bear kept going faster and faster.

As they raced through a moonlit clearing, the prospector looked down at his mount.

"My God!" he exclaimed. "I'm on the wrong bear!"

View of taxidermic black bears. 1890 (Courtesy Colorado Historical Society Call No. CHS.X6762)

"Return of the Bear Hunters, Navajo" Photo by Ben Wittick 1880
(Courtesy Museum of New Mexico Neg. No 015931)

The Missing Hunter

Many years ago, according to a Navajo legend, there was a young Navajo maiden named Morning Star who had two suitors, Flying Arrow and Falling Rocks. She couldn't decide which of these two young men to marry, so she asked her father, a wise old man of the tribe if he had any suggestions.

Her father said she should marry the man who could prove himself to be the best provider and suggested a contest.

"Let each man arm himself with a bow and arrow and let them set out at sunrise to look for game," he said. "The man who returns first with fresh meat should be the one you should marry."

Both Flying Arrow and Falling Rocks agreed to the contest, and at sunrise on the designated day, each picked up a bow and arrows and started off in different directions. Before sunset, Flying Arrow returned, dragging a freshly killed deer.

"Flying Arrow has won the contest, and he is the man you should marry," Morning Star's father told her. She agreed, but said she didn't want to commit herself until she could see what Falling Rocks brought in.

One day went by, then another, and another, but there was no sign of Falling Rocks. After a week or two, when Falling Rocks still had not returned, Morning Star became quite worried, and organized a Navajo search party to go look for him. The search parties fanned out in all directions, scouring mountains, mesas and canyons in a vain hunt for a trace of Falling Rocks.

The search continues even today, the legend says, and each time the Navajo searchers cross a mountain highway in northern New Mexico or Arizona, they erect a sign asking motorists to "Watch For Falling Rocks."

Unidentified Indian man squatting and smoking a peace pipe Photo by D.F. Barry (Courtesy Denver Public Library Call No. B-401)

Chief San Juan and Mescalero Apache Indians 1883 Photo by Edwin A. Bass (Courtesy Museum of New Mexico Neg. No. 090634)

Peace Pipe Warning

This story was related by the late Wendell Chino, president of the Mescalero Apache Tribe. A male tourist visited a Mescalero Apache arts and crafts shop on the New Mexico reservation, and after examining all the crafts, decided to buy a handcrafted Apache peace pipe. He stood for a while admiring the beautiful woodwork and featherwork on his purchase, then noticed that there was something written in the Apache language on the stem.

"What does that say?" the tourist asked the Apache clerk.

"Oh, nothing important," the Indian replied.

"Look, I paid a lot of money for this peace pipe, and I think I have a right to know the meaning of those Apache words on the stem," the tourist said.

With that, the clerk took the peace pipe from the customer, examined the stem, and translated the Apache words as follows:

Warning. The surgeon general has determined that smoking is dangerous to your health.

First daily newspaper, Kingston, New Mexico, 1886 Photo by J. C. Burge
(Courtesy Museum of New Mexico Neg. No. 014691)

SOME EXAMPLES OF FRONTIER HUMOR

As Published In Early Newspapers

A suspicious mother in Las Vegas placed some nitroglycerine in her daughter's corset on the evening her fellow was coming. The girl loaned them to the cook, and they had to scrape the old man off the ceiling to get enough of him to hold an inquest. (Albuquerque Evening Review, May 19, 1881)

A highly unlikely story, but a prime example of some of the tall tales, exaggerations, jokes and fabrications that early New Mexico newspapers often published as short news items for the entertainment of their readers.

Just as unlikely was an article that appeared in an 1887 issue of Arizona's *Tombstone Epitaph* that was reprinted in an Albuquerque newspaper that year without comment:

An Albuquerque, New Mexico editor, who expected a gang of lynchers to come for him about the middle of the night, took himself to the cellar, leaving a pet grizzly bear in his place instead. The lynchers did not bring any light, but made a plucky attempt to get out the bear and lynch it, but gave it up after three of them had lost an eye apiece, two of them had suffered the loss of thumbs chewed off, and the other six were more or less deprived of skin. The editor now has a great reputation as a fighter, and the bear did not mind the work one bit.

Possible, but probably not entirely true, was this item from an 1882 issue of the Albuquerque *Evening Review*:

> *At the railroad boarding house in San Marcial there is a young lady who waits on the table with a revolver in hand. She offers the soup, and if refused, she presents the revolver, when they generally change their minds and accept.*

Early newspapers were often critical of what they considered rival newspapers even if they were in different localities. The establishment of a newspaper in the railroad community of Wallace, now the village of Domingo between Albuquerque and Santa Fe, prompted this item in the Albuquerque *Evening Review*:

> *The well known Padre Aoy and George Albright are running the Wallace Watchman. The Padre is in his dotage, and George is brainless, but the Watchman is printed on very fine white paper and is recommended to housekeepers as a covering for preserve jars. (February 20, 1882)*

Community rivalry also found its place in the newspapers, such as this brief item in an 1883 issue of the Deming *Headlight*:

> *Water has been struck in a railroad well near Lordsburg, and there is talk of the people there experimenting with that fluid as a beverage.*

The Grant County *Herald*, an early Silver City *Weekly*, had an odd habit of poking fun at local citizens who had been injured in accidents. Here are three examples:

> *Mr. James Nottingham, whilst traveling in a stagecoach in Texas, on a sideling road, thoughtlessly changed his quid of tobacco to the nether cheek, thereby causing the overturning of the coach, which resulted in serious injury to himself. (December 12, 1875)*

John Huff was attacked by a well bucket. It went for him about midway of the well to the bottom, where John was earning his daily bread by blasting, picking and shoveling. The bucket got John down, cut a great gash in his head, and not withstanding, we have no report of the arrest of the bucket for aggravated assault. When John has sufficiently convalesced, he can do no less, if he has the sand in his craw, to kick its bottom -- out. (August 27, 1875)

Colonel R.B. Willison on Thursday night when not even a star twinkled in the heavens was attempting to cross the breast of the dam, missed his footing and fell a distance of perhaps ten feet and was followed by a boulder which he dislodged in his descent and which hit him plump in the back. He was considerably bruised in every part except his eye winkers, and his knee suffered most in consequence of the ineffectual attempt to drill a hole in the rock. Perhaps the colonel now thinks that nothing is gained by short cuts across lots except for an anxious desire for a better knowledge of pharmacy. (August 29, 1875)

The Silver City paper also found amusement in a local minister's attempt to conduct a religious service in the nearby mining community of Georgetown:

Sunday last the Rev. C.W. Stewart turned up in Georgetown and tried to snatch a few brands from the burning, but a bully boy with a chrystaline eye -- we may say several -- who were present, didn't kitten to his teachings worth a cent, and consequently the preacher, like a clam shell, was obliged to shut up before he had half unwound firstly. (June 20, 1875

Condensing news articles into the fewest possible words also was common among frontier journalists, such as this item from an 1881 issue of the Albuquerque *Evening Review*:

Curly, the noted highwayman of Deadwood, argued with two officers who were taking him to jail that as he had the fleetest horse he could put spurs to him and escape. They told him that bullets would riddle him before he could get out of range, and when he suddenly undertook to demonstrate his theory, they verified the correctness of theirs.

Or this brief item from the Silver City *Enterprise*:

Black Pete, the noted horse thief and rustler, was found dead near Savoya with a bullet in his head. The coroner's jury returned a verdict like this: Killed by a thunderbolt from heaven. (June 6, 1884)

A headline in the Las Vegas *Optic* over an 1881 article about Apache warfare in southern New Mexico read: "Our Naughty Neighbors, Ushering Souls Into Eternity by the Tomahawk." An 1884 headline in the same newspaper read: "A Brave Man, John McCabe, the Pimp, Beats a Woman Over the Head with a Slungshot, A Dastardly Deed Which Calls For Quick Action by the Law, Or Somebody."

The editor of a Las Cruces weekly called *Thirty Four*, in a bound volume of these newspapers for the year 1878. Handwritten on the flyleaf of the bound volume were these words:

The editor must not be held responsible for all the bad grammar to be found in this bound volume; for, while he has been the factotum of the office and has been compelled by poverty to not only do the writing and reporting, but also to act as office boy, pressman, carrier, devil and cook, he has at times been compelled to leave the office in temporary charge of some printer hired for the occasion, in order to make business trips around the country.

Silver City, Broadway near Hudson Street, The building at right housed the
Silver City Enterprise & Southwest Sentinel newspaper offices prior to 1895
Photo by Silver City Daily Press(Courtesy Silver City Museum Neg. No. 492)

> *During these absences his 'substitute' has frequently butchered*
> *the English language in such a barbarous fashion as to shock the*
> *sensibilities of anyone pretending to even a slight acquaintance*
> *with the rules of rhetoric laid down by Lindley Murray. Some*
> *of these butcheries are to be found in the issues of ... [Dates of*
> *issues then given.]*

When Hezekiah S. Johnson, an Albuquerque lawyer, launched publication of an Albuquerque weekly newspaper called the *Rio Abajo Press*
on January 20, 1863, he explained to readers in a front page editorial
that the paper would charge for circulation and advertising as "we have
not yet arrived at that state of beatified transcendentalism that pro-
duces repugnance to the almighty dollar."

Libel suits against early newspapers were rare, as most frontier
newspapers were low on cash, and those who thought they were li-
beled or slandered often preferred to settle their differences with their
fists. A prime example of a quick apology was found by a Montana

publisher, who while researching through the early files of the Lewistown Argus, found the following headlines over an article about the arrest of an alleged horse thief:

DIRTY HORSE THIEF CAUGHT RED HANDED WITH THE GOODS.

Will Probably Be Strung Up and Good Riddance.

Stole Horse From Defenseless Widow.

A jury acquitted the man of the charge the next day, and the same newspaper published the article under these headlines:

HIGHLY RESPECTED CITIZEN WRONGLY ACCUSED OF THEFT.

Stupid Charge Embarrasses Man.

Widow Was Out To Get Him on False Charges.

New Mexico's first English language newspaper was the Santa Fe *Republican*, which began publication on September 10, 1847, with Edward T. Davis as editor. It was succeeded two years later by *the New Mexican*, which began publication on November 24, 1849, with the same editor and press of its predecessor.

Since that time, approximately 1300 newspapers have been published in about 200 New Mexico communities, some lasting only a few weeks, and others, like *the New Mexican*, Las Vegas *Optic* and Albuquerque *Journal*, lasting more than a century.

Portion of Santa Fe Daily Democrat, Wednesday October 13, 1880
(Courtesy of author's collection)

INDEX

H

I

J

K

L

Howard Bryan Photograph © Marcia Keegan

HOWARD BRYAN, a nationally-recognized authority on New Mexico history, has been chronicling Western adventures in this state for over fifty years and is still going strong. His latest book, *Santa Fe Tales & More*, will offer a wealth of fascinating true stories of old Santa Fe. As is his custom, he will tell the city's stories with plenty of local color and bits of humor while maintaining a meticulous standard of accuracy.

A veteran New Mexico journalist and historical writer, Bryan was a well-known reporter and columnist for the Albuquerque Tribune from 1948 to 1990. When he began working for the Tribune, he developed a passion for New Mexico history and culture—especially forgotten stories buried in 19th century newspaper archives and the treasures to be found in the living memories of New Mexico oldtimers. These rich resources were the basis for his thousands of columns and articles as well as his books on the wilder aspects of the New Mexico frontier.

As a popular historical writer, Bryan has sought out the odd, unusual and little-known facts and anecdotes of the Old West. His informality and dry wit have won him many admirers over the years, and he has been featured on several network television programs, including appearances on The Real West series on the Arts and Entertainment Network.

Bryan is author of four other critically acclaimed non-fiction books: *True Tales of the American Southwest*, *Wildest of the Wild West*, *Incredible Elfego Baca* and *Robbers, Rogues and Ruffians*, all detailing the stories of some Wild West characters of the frontier era. *Incredible Elfego Baca* won a 1994 Spur Award from the Western Writers of America as the best short western nonfiction book of the year.

During his 42-year career as a journalist, Howard Bryan received various New Mexico Press awards, and in 1994 he was awarded the Governor's Award for Excellence and Achievement in the Arts. His great knowledge of New Mexico history, coupled with his genius for storytelling and his dry wit, have won him a large following over the years. He is a long-time resident of Albuquerque.